The Best Guided Walking Tours
of New York City
For Residents and Visitors

The Best Guided Walking Tours of New York City For Residents and Visitors

Exploring the Neighborhoods of Manhattan and Other Boroughs

by Leslie Gourse

A Voyager Book

The Globe Pequot Press

Chester, Connecticut

Prices and schedules of tours listed in this book were confirmed at press time. We recommend, however, that you call ahead to obtain the most current information, as tours vary considerably not only in price but in route, starting points, and availability.

All photographs by the author, except pages 135 and 155 (courtesy of the New York Convention and Visitors Bureau), and page 181 (courtesy of the Brooklyn Historical Society).

Cover design by Laura M. Pollack
Cover photography of city skyline by Tony Sitsch and Washington Square photography by Leslie Gourse

Library of Congress Cataloging-in-Publication Data

Gourse, Leslie.
    "A Voyager Book"
    The best guided walking tours of New York City for residents and visitors / by Leslie Gourse.—
1st ed.
        p.   cm.
    Includes index.
    ISBN 0-87106-637-8
    1. New York (N.Y.)—Description—1989- —Tours. 2. Walking—New York (N.Y.)—Guide-books. I. Title.
F128.18.G65 1989
917.47'10443—dc19   89-2044
                                                                 CIP

Manufactured in the United States of America
First Edition/First Printing

Contents

List of Maps

Chapter One

Walking Tours—
Your Key to the City

Seventeen million visitors come to New York City every year, and an enormous travel and tourism industry serves them. The New York Convention and Visitors Bureau has two midtown offices, one at 59th Street and Columbus Circle, the other at Times Square between Broadway and Seventh Avenue. They dispense brochures on tours and events in addition to book-sized pamphlets on hotel/tour packages. But neither the brochures nor the pamphlets cover the vast repertoire of walking tours, which have been gaining in popularity for more than three decades. If you ask at the desks of the tourist centers, you may find out about only a couple of tours.

Lucky, curious, or adventuresome tourists discover the hundreds of walking tours presented by free-lance guides, lecturers, institutions, associations, vacation firms, and special-interest groups through ads in the media, flyers, travel agencies, hotel tour services, organized conventions, or by word of mouth along a grapevine of friends familiar with New York City's myriad cultural offerings. Local newspapers frequently publish stories about some of the outstanding tours or leaders. The 92nd Street YMHA/YWHA alone offers about 200 walking tours every year; some utilize the talents of New York City's elite cadre of professional leaders. These leaders usually have college degrees in such subjects as sociology, American civilization, the natural sciences, law, economics, communications, and history. After receiving their degrees, these guides have gone on to teach themselves about the city by habitual sight-seeing and avid reading on New York's history, music, art, architecture, literature, economics, politics, sociology, planning—every facet of the town, even its geological composition—until they can spout facts the way sportscasters remember statistics.

Regarding the structure of this book, it first provides sketches of the leading guides and then describes the best-established and interesting walking tours in Manhattan, mentions tours in other boroughs, and finally suggests tours by subjects that are not confined to one neighborhood. While it might take you years on your own to delve into the city's mysterious charms, a few well-chosen tours can sensitize you to the evolution of the metropolis, its fascinating operations, and its intrigues. When you visit the NBC newsroom, the Metropolitan Opera House's backstage, or historic Wall Street, Greenwich Village, Upper Broadway, or the Upper East Side on organized tours with experts, you'll quickly experience the dynamism of the city, the layers of her history, and the majesty of her people's achievements.

Enduring Popularity

Something about New York City lends itself to walking tours, which have been popular for decades. Architectural historian Henry Hope Reed and painter E. Powis Jones initiated some of the first of those tours in 1955 under the auspices of the Municipal Art Society (M.A.S.), a preservationist group. By 1960 the Museum of the City of New York, which still has one of the city's most prestigious walking-tour series, expanded the Reed-Jones concept and instituted walking tours as a regular museum feature. Reed and Jones concentrated on New York's architectural history, emphasizing above all the classical forms of the city's most beautiful buildings. A few years later, the M. A. S. put a full-fledged tour program into operation, too.

Parisians have long been devoted to their arrondissements and have proudly regaled visitors with minute historical details. Londoners, too, have traditionally sponsored walking tours daily, sometimes hourly, from the tube stations around their history-laden city. These cities became civilizations in themselves centuries ago. Now New York, the youngest and fastest-developing of the great Western metropolises, has joined them. By the time walking tours started in New York, New Yorkers had developed preservationist passions for their favorite neighborhoods, along with a great appreciation of, and curiosity about, the city's architecture, arts, history, and legends. In fact, New Yorkers themselves became the biggest fans of the walks, which constituted mini-vacations for many of them, offering an escape from the stresses of daily routines. New Yorkers living in cramped quarters could expand their horizons and dream their dreams without ever leaving their home town. Of course, tourists, for whom the tours were in large part invented, like them as well.

Tour audiences usually see a small portion of the city at a time, though walking tours occasionally combine bus and walking forays, especially those tours concerning architecture, jazz sites, famous rendezvous for lovers, or sites of historic crimes. Unlike bus tours, which are also popular, walking tours give people a chance to linger and savor details. Bus tours can skim the awesome landscape from Harlem to historic Wall Street, from Broadway to the United Nations, in a single morning and sometimes add to a visitor's sense of being overwhelmed. On walking tours, one gets a chance to learn something special about the city on a small scale and to meet other people. Indeed, walking tours often afford strangers the chance to mingle, chat amiably, and even sit down together for a meal along the way. The New York Historical Society, for one, has found that its receptions, with coffee and cookies following the tours, are very popular. Altogether, a sense of shared discoveries makes communal walking tours entertaining little caravans.

Walking-tour season never ceases entirely, even in very cold and snowy weather. One early spring tour group in 1988 ducked into a few bank foyers to warm up, the members admitting themselves with their bank cards for the automatic teller machines. Though sizable groups do show up for the relatively few tours that are scheduled in cold weather, tour season generally runs from mid-March through mid-November.

Every Which Way You Look

Tours visit every nook and cranny of New York City, where each guide puts his or her personal stamp on the views. The differences between tours in the same neighborhoods reside in each guide's focus, expertise or emphasis, personal interest, viewpoint, or prejudice, as well as the historical period highlighted by the tour. A variety of tours stress a neighborhood's architecture, socioeconomic development, cultural cachet, Colonial or pre-Colonial roots, nineteenth-century development, current or past ethnic orientation—or all of those aspects.

Most tours are aptly named. For example, "Noshing in New York," led by Lou Singer, owner of Singer's Tours, covers the ethnic restaurants on the Lower East Side and in Greenwich Village. Joseph Schiff's "The World of Our Fathers" tour covers the Lower East Side, stressing Jewish culture. Professor James Shenton calls one of his favorite tours "Irish New York."

The institutions and private guides often provide brochures or flyers explaining the orientation of their tours. Private guides will custom-tailor tours for groups of all sizes.

Tours of all lengths and for all prices are available. A few tours, usually regularly scheduled ones such as the Wednesday noontime walks around Grand Central Terminal and hikes through the city parks, are subsidized and are free of charge to the public. Most tours under the auspices of cultural institutions cost under $10 per person. When freelancers with their own firms negotiate package terms directly with groups, fees can range from $5 to $10 per person up to $500 for a whole group for a full day.

The Guides—Fonts of Knowledge

Walking-tour guides are a special cadre of New Yorkers. While a few of the best came from other cities, such as Chicago, many are native New Yorkers. All the guides have become fascinated with and knowledgeable about New York City and take their guide work quite seriously. They jump in to fill the void in the lives of tourists—who might otherwise get lost—and make the city a more substantial and comprehensible place for New Yorkers as well.

At their best, as they explain some of the city's beauties and eccentricities, and expose some of its contradictions, the guides can remind you of the little child who cried out that the emperor had no clothes. For example, Michael Levin leads an offbeat tour of the artsy Soho district, where he emphasizes how overpriced the nonart fashions and food are: as proof, he shows you $150 polyester jackets and $40-a-pound salad greens. He goes on to explain why a neighborhood like Soho thrives in old, crowded, battered, utility-and-celebrity-conscious New York City better than in any other place in the United States.

Guides such as Levin, who are impassioned city buffs, present walking tours amounting to street theater and universities-without-walls combined. These committed guides invent their own walking-tour routes, employ visual aids—especially antique photographs and drawings—and fill their lectures with choice bits of information acquired from painstaking studies. Many guides are generalists, able to talk for hours about each of the city's neighborhoods (primarily those in Manhattan). Some guides are specialists, with expertise about particular neighborhoods or aspects of them. Some guides are more accurate than others about exact dates, events, and names. Anecdotes occasionally blur historic facts. But the spirit of the city's vitality remains intact or, even better, is underscored.

The public can find out about tours in various ways. Free-lance guides may put notices in the myriad papers and weekly magazines circulating in New York City. Travel agencies, and especially convention groups, aware of the value and popularity of walking tours, offer them to out-of-towners visiting New York City for conventions or on packaged vacations. Hotels often leave leaflets about tours for their guests. Established cultural institutions hire seasoned guides with excellent reputations for organized walking-tour programs; schedules are often planned a year in advance and advertised in newspapers shortly preceding each walk.

Guides are usually very quick walkers; they will linger for a while in one spot, while they deliver their lectures, and then walk at a good clip to the next site. They're also adept at crossing hectic streets. And they can pitch their voices to project to a large crowd. Furthermore, they never seem to tire; though they notice that most people like two-hour tours and then want to rest, the guides themselves usually feel fresh for at least three hours and sometimes for a whole day. Walking tours can last from two hours to a full day or even an overnight foray. If you're not a long-distance walker, or only have a short time to spend on a walking tour, check the schedules before you set out.

Walking Tours

Marvin Gelfand, a professional guide with his own tour company, Walk of the Town, recalls leading a tour of the Upper West Side along Upper Broadway. He started leading forty people on a walk scheduled for two hours and ended up walking and talking for four hours: "I kept ducking into side streets, synagogues, churches, and I talked about all the writers who lived in the neighborhoods: A. J. Liebling, Damon Runyon," he says. "I talked about hotels, apartment houses, everything! I'm long-winded, and a walking tour is a concentrated experience. You find out a great deal in a brief time. At the end of my tour, twenty-five people were still with me."

It's not unusual, however, for tours to stretch beyond their assigned time limit without anyone dropping out of the ranks. For the hardy, Val Ginter, who also has his own firm, Ginter Gotham Urban History, has devised what he calls "The Ultimate Greenwich Village Tour," and all-day affair that begins in the East Village near 14th Street and ends in the winding little "Far West" Village streets a short distance from the Hudson River. Actually, the distance covered isn't very great in miles, but the historic, social, and cultural territory covered is enormous. Time passes quickly when the sights are tantalizing and the lectures humorous and elucidating.

Some guides specialize in neighborhoods outside of Manhattan. Justin Ferate has a reputation as a Brooklyn specialist, though he can also lead tours in some areas of Manhattan expertly. Joe Zito, a retired New York City police captain, became fascinated with the Hell's Kitchen neighborhood in Manhattan a long time ago. Now he leads the quintessential tour of that area. Cy Adler is an expert on the city's shorelines and leads at least one marathon tour along the Hudson every year. The New York City Park Rangers are knowledgeable about the city's parklands; some Rangers have special expertise about aspects of nature. One Park Ranger, who speaks Chinese, is the Ranger of choice for a rare, parks-sponsored tour of Columbus Park in Chinatown.

Not a formal group but a loose gathering of city buffs, a band of tour leaders that calls itself "The New Amsterdam Antiquarian Chowder and Marching Society" meets every last Thursday of the month at 6:00 P.M. for dinner at Donohue's restaurant on W. 72nd Street near the southeast corner of Broadway. A long wooden table is set aside that night by

7

Donohue's. Anyone who shows up is welcome to join the group. Usually the diners are tour leaders and members of the press.

"We share a personal enthusiasm for New York City," says Marvin Gelfand, who attends the dinners regularly. "No one else but each other shares our mania. You say: 'Rudolph Valentino had his funeral at St. Malachy's on 49th Street,' and only the gray heads and the people here know what you're talking about." The group fancies itself a version of the Algonquin Hotel's legendary Literary Roundtable.

The group came into being after Barry Lewis, a native of Queens, emerged as a force in the growing movement of tours that teach New York City history in a way it was never taught in the classroom. Lewis's expertise, which was primarily self-acquired, became sought after by students of the city in the 1970s, as varied walking tours began proliferating. In 1977 the Municipal Art Society, housed in the palatial, landmark Villard Houses on Madison Avenue in midtown, hired Lewis to give a unique course called "The City Transformed" on the city's development, architecture, and planning. The M. A. S. already had a guide-training program at the time.

Lewis's M. A. S. lectures, augmented by slides, were fact-filled and exciting. He alternated his classroom sessions with walking tours for the intellectually curious guides-in-training and city buffs. Afterward, he accompanied many of his students to dinners for more talk about the Big Apple. These dinners took place all over Manhattan and even in Brooklyn, Queens, and the Bronx, in all types of ethnic restaurants. By the mid-1980s, the dinner regulars, including many alumni of the Lewis course, settled down to a routine of meeting at Donohue's, an old Irish pub with lumpy banquettes. They are equaled, for informal ambience, by the restaurant's dim lighting and plain cuisine. Characteristically, the guides who gather here for the dinners are very impressed by the fact that the two policemen who solved a famous Upper West Side murder case—the "Mr. Goodbar" case—used to drink here. The aura of that tidbit of gossip is positively as spicy as the steak sauce for the guides.

These urban historians, with varied emphases, depending on their expertise, are an excellent source of information about what good tours are taking place in town. Sooner or later, many of the city's elite guides make an appearance here for a dinner. For conversation, these historians-without-portfolios, whose only subject is New York City and anything pertinent to it (ranging from other states' laws to the nation's rail system, to the Beaux Arts School of Architecture in Paris, to international migration routes) can embroider entertainingly on subjects written about concisely and drily, if written about at all, in books or in monographs or in the official literature of the city's Landmarks Commission.

The guides would like more credit for their specialized work. "The *New York Times* prints a notice that a tour will be held but never says who is giving it," says Joyce Mendelsohn, a public-school teacher who prefers her moonlighting job as a guide. She invented an overnight walk that takes place on July 4 in the historic Wall Street area, accompanied by police escort and sponsored by the 92nd Street "Y." Actually the papers do sometimes write stories about individual guides and their tours, but occasionally the tours are announced while the guides remain anonymous. "My problem," says Ms. Mendelsohn, "is to raise the consciousness that tours are as important as lectures in schools."

Sometimes guides at the dinner refer tour dates they cannot keep to their "Roundtable" friends. Or a guide might speculate about how much money another guide (not present at the table that night) is earning. Some tours meet with high praise, others with subtle disdain. "She must have bought some mailing lists from museums and is charging whopping prices for a museum tour, walking from picture to picture . . ." speculated one experienced guide, as an example of the professionals' self-scrutiny and the standards they set for themselves.

Chapter Two

Sponsoring Guides, Firms, and Institutions

The institutions, firms, and professional guides offering tours in New York City are described below in alphabetical order. All guides or tour sponsors are generalists, visiting most Manhattan neighborhoods, unless noted by one star as specialists. All phone numbers are in the Manhattan and Bronx *212* area code, unless otherwise specified as *718* for Brooklyn, Queens, and Staten Island; *516* for Long Island's Nassau and Suffolk counties; *609* for Princeton, New Jersey; and *914* for Westchester County, New York. For all numbers outside the *212* area code, dial *1* first. Single tours costing more than $10 per person have two stars.

The following thumbnail sketches describe the overall work of the guides and tour sponsors. Specific tours are delineated in the chapters organized by neighborhoods that follow.

Adventure on a Shoestring
Howard Goldberg, founder and owner
300 E. 53rd Street, New York, NY 10019
265–2663.

Mr. Goldberg organizes tours for members who pay annual membership fees of less than $50 to visit interesting sites or performances in and around New York City. His group began when he was told, years ago, that he could visit the *Herald Tribune* newsroom if he arrived with a tour group. He advertised the tour in a newspaper and elicited such a resounding response that he formed his firm and began to organize tours regularly. He has varied destinations—museums, the Metropolitan Opera's backstage, and Chinatown, to name a few. Most tours take place in Manhattan. Many are open to the public for a small fee.

American Museum of Natural History
Central Park West at 79th Street, New York, NY 10024
873-1300
*

The museum offers walking tours of its own exhibits. Dr. Sidney Horenstein, a staff geologist, also schedules some tours independent of his museum work, to study the geological composition of the city's buildings and parks, including that of the museum itself. Professor Horenstein's private office phone number is 569-5351.

Art Deco Society of New York
145 Hudson Street, 7th floor, New York, NY 10013
925-4946
*

The society schedules tours of the city's art deco highlights. For example, the Chrysler Building, at 405 Lexington Avenue between E. 42nd and E. 43rd streets, is one of New York's most notable art deco structures. Radio City Music Hall is part of the Rockefeller Center art deco urban masterpiece. And another art deco treasure is the Empire State Building. The Art Deco Society visits these and many other art deco buildings on tours intended to aid in the preservation and appreciation of art deco by the public.

Art Tours of Manhattan
76 Library Place, Princeton, NJ 08540
609-683-0881
Also, 63 E. 82nd Street, New York, NY 10028
*/**

Under the auspices of art historian Barbara Guggenheim, this firm leads custom-tailored tours of art schools, museums, galleries, and artists' lofts and studios, which include talks by art dealers and art experts. Sometimes the firm stages a lecture with a slide show and catered reception in its 82nd Street townhouse headquarters, before proceeding with a tour of a museum's show.

Backstage on Broadway
Mr. Lloyd Meeke, director
228 W. 47th Street, New York, NY 10036
575–8065
*

This firm schedules daytime tours, with lectures on the operations of a Broadway theater, Mondays through Saturdays at 10:30 A.M. Professionals involved in the production of shows give the lectures. Tours usually visit the Edison or Helen Hayes theaters, occasionally others. Call first and show up at the assigned theater.

"Wild Man" Steve Brill
718–291–6825
Or c/o New York City Department of Parks and Recreation
830 Fifth Avenue, New York, NY 10021
360–8165
*

Mr. Brill became famous when he was arrested in 1986 for leading tours, for fees, through Central Park, pointing out edible weeds. Charges were dismissed, and this self-taught naturalist was then hired by the city's Parks Department to lead legal, free tours for the public of the following city parks: Central, Inwood, Riverside, and Fort Tryon parks in Manhattan; Marine and Prospect parks in Brooklyn; the Green Belt System on Staten Island; Forest, Alley Pond, Flushing Meadow, Kissena, and Cunningham parks, and Jamaica Bay in the Rockaway area in Queens; and Van Cortlandt, Pelham Bay, and Bronx River parks in the Bronx.

He also gives a course in the theory of field botany, leads walks in New Jersey, Long Island, Connecticut, and Pennsylvania, and gives lectures about his hobby-turned-career. You must reserve a place on Mr. Brill's tours, which are free to the public in the city parks. No smoking is allowed. Inquire about his field-botany course when you call him.

Bronx Historical Society
3309 Bainbridge Avenue, Bronx, NY 10467
881–8900
*

Walking tours usually take place on Saturdays, occasionally on Sundays. Some tours cross the Bronx, while others go into the borough's parks or along the Bronx Heritage Trail. Tours visit the South Bronx and Bedford Park for their art deco architecture. And once a year, the society sponsors a tour on horseback and another by boat.

Brooklyn Historical Society
128 Pierrepont Street, Brooklyn, NY 11201
718–624–0890
*

Free-lance guides lead tours from March to November, with special tours for schoolchildren. Destinations include Fort Hamilton; Brighton Beach, where the new Russian Jewish immigrants have created "Little Odessa" and the vodka flows like wine at Sunday-afternoon parties in restaurants; Sheepshead Bay, a fishing community with early-morning boat departures daily; Fulton Ferry Landing; Fort Greene; Clinton Mill; Flatbush, with its long, colorful history; and the ethnically diverse Bay Ridge. Guides are often **Justin Ferate** and **John Kriskiewicz;** Kriskiewicz works primarily in Brooklyn, occasionally in Manhattan.

Chinatown History Project
70 Mulberry Street, 2nd floor, New York, NY 10013
619–4785
*

The project is funded as an information resource, complete with a library about the Chinese-American community in the United States from its beginnings in the mid-nineteenth century. Walking tours are scheduled daily and include a thirty-minute slide show and sixty-minute stroll through New York's fastest-growing enclave. The tours and shows make Chinatown a comprehensible, as well as a fascinating, spectacle.

Sponsoring Guides

Classical America
Box 821, Times Square Station, New York, NY 10108
*

Founded by Henry Hope Reed, this organization is dedicated to encouraging an appreciation and a renaissance of premodernist expression in all the arts.

Mr. Reed has written two books on the grandeur of classical architecture and classical forms in art: *The Golden City* and *The New York Public Library: Its Architecture and Decoration,* both published by W. W. Norton Co. *The Golden City,* which has many photographs comparing classical and modern New York City buildings, provides a surprisingly persuasive argument for Mr. Reed's messianic point of view. And those New York City guides who are aware of his early leadership, whether they agree with his point of view or not, regard him with appreciation as the "Father of the Walking Tour" in New York City.

With painter E. Powis Jones, Mr. Reed started some walking tours for the Municipal Art Society in 1955 and, by 1960, moved them as a regular program to the Museum of the City of New York. The walks inspired many New York City buffs to devise their own tours and turn a pastime into a thriving Manhattan tourist industry. **Michael George,** a CBS newsman who also teaches about New York City architectural highlights at New York University, leads several tours every year for Classical America. Write to the group for its annual tour schedule.

Columbia University
c/o Lewisohn Hall, #418
116th Street and Broadway, New York, NY 10027,
Attn: Mr. J. Kissone
280–2838
*/**

Columbia sponsors walking tours as part of several courses on art, history, and architecture. The best-known tour leader is **Dr. James Shenton,** a history professor who began leading walking tours in New York City as part of his lectures about the Civil War draft riots of 1865. He has expanded his tour program to cover about a dozen neighbor-

hoods in Brooklyn, the Bronx, and Queens, as well as Manhattan.
Also under the aegis of Columbia, Adjunct Assistant Professor of Art
Donald Reynolds leads architectural tours of New York, and Andrew
Dolkart, Adjunct Assistant Professor of Architecture, takes groups to see
examples of buildings from historical periods in town—a Dutch Colonial
farmhouse, cast-iron buildings, nineteenth-century brownstones, and
others—as part of an introductory course. The general public may join
in the walking tours on a single day's basis, though they are quite expensive that way.

Columbia also offers a less expensive "Encore Series" of events,
including walking tours. As part of this series, Dr. Shenton leads walks
to Chinatown and Little Italy, to the Lower East Side to explore the
traces of Jewish life that once flourished there, and to the section of the
Lower East Side that once constituted Irish New York. These destinations are among Dr. Shenton's favorite areas for tours.

Libby Corydon
369–0954
A full-time travel executive and free-lance tour leader who conducts
multilingual bus tours, Libby Corydon also offers walking tours in many
city neighborhoods. Two of her favorites are Harlem and Lower Manhattan's historic district. From Lower Manhattan, she likes to lead tours at
dusk across the Brooklyn Bridge to Brooklyn Heights, from where she
can easily point out the brightly lit, historic harbor of Manhattan. Ms.
Corydon majored in American civilization in college and spent several
years studying and working in Europe, where she learned to speak
French, German, and Dutch. She feels that she's returning the hospital-
ity to visitors in New York City that they extended to her.

Doorway to Design
1441 Broadway, Suite 338, New York, NY 10018
221–1111 (days); 718–339–1543 (evenings)
*/**
This firm, run by Sheila Sperber, sponsors tours of Greenwich Village with visits to private houses and studios, as well as walks around

Sponsoring Guides

Gramercy Park and Brooklyn Heights, with special attention to the art and design in the neighborhoods.

Federal Reserve Bank of New York
33 Liberty Street, New York, NY 10048
720–6130
*This tour is free of charge.

The bank requires at least one week's advance reservation for a tour of its operations, given Mondays through Fridays at 10:00 A.M., 11:00 A.M., 1:00 P.M., and 2:00 P.M. You will hear a talk about the bank's security system, see money being counted and shredded, view a collection of historic coins, and, as the highlight, visit the underground gold vault, the largest in the world.

Justin Ferate
208 Adelphi Street, Brooklyn, NY 11205
718–625–7413

A Brooklyn specialist, Mr. Ferate is also a generalist in Manhattan and works full-time as a guide for cultural institutions and special groups.

Brooklyn highlights in Mr. Ferate's repertoire include: the country-like mansions of Flatbush; the Sheepshead Bay fishing community; the Brighton Beach Russian community and the elevated subway train to the beach; Park Slope's nineteenth-century architecture; Brooklyn Heights, which was New York City's first designated historic-landmark district; Stuyvesant Heights, with its nineteenth-century row houses; the Brooklyn Museum, with one of the finest Egyptian collections in the world and an American paintings collection of great note; the Botanical Gardens; Bay Ridge, an Italian-Irish-Greek-Chinese neighborhood above the Verrazano Narrows Bridge; Prospect Park, designed by Olmsted and Vaux, architects of Central Park; Clinton Hill's mansion; and a Coney Island sideshow.

Mr. Ferate's expertise ranges from the historic Wall Street area to Harlem in Manhattan and extends to Riverdale, the Wave Hill Gardens, opened under the authority of the city's Department of Parks and Recreation, and City Island in the Bronx.

Friends of Central Park
16 E. 8th Street, New York, NY 10003
473-6283
*

A group dedicated to preserving parkland, Friends of Central Park has been charging $1 for its annual extravaganza, typically an overnight walk through Harlem; from Manhattan's West Side through the Hudson Tubes to New Jersey; or across the Brooklyn Bridge. These walks usually end with an outdoor picnic. The group also sponsors shorter walks throughout the year; for example, a daytime hike through Greenwich Village. Aside from walking tours, the group distributes information and magazines on matters of interest to naturalists and horticulturists and organizes vacations outside of New York City. Write for information.

Marvin Gelfand's Walk of the Town
280 Riverside Drive, New York, NY 10025
222-5343
Marvin Gelfand, who leads tours for his own firm as well as for major cultural institutions, holds degrees in economics. Gelfand specializes in tours of the Wall Street area; Jewish Harlem and the Jewish Lower East Side; rendezvous of famous lovers and the sites of historic crimes; and the Upper West Side and parts of Brooklyn. He will lead custom-tailored tours on request by the public.

Michael George, c/o CBS Television Network News
524 W. 57th Street, New York, NY 10019
975-4114
Or c/o Classical America (see address above)
Private number: 662-2597
A well-known, veteran New York City tour leader and an architectural historian, Mr. George can take a tour group on any block in town and deliver an insightful talk on both the history of Manhattan and the culture of the neighborhood from clues provided by the architecture. Mr. George leads seven to ten tours annually for Classical America, an organization that stresses the beauty of pre-Modernist architecture—a point of view in which Mr. George concurs. He also works as a free-lancer for

19

independent groups and for major cultural institutions, including the 92nd Street "Y," the New York Historical Society, and New York University's School of Continuing Education, where he teaches classes about the city's architecture and takes students on tours to illustrate his lectures. He has served on the board of directors of the Municipal Art Society, for whom, with guide Val Ginter, he designed a walking tour of Grand Central Terminal; the tour helped preserve the terminal from demolition and make it a historic landmark protected by law. George calls New York City an encyclopedia of architecture dating back more than 300 years, and he reads the encyclopedia on the buildings' facades and makes them exciting for tourists.

Ginter-Gotham Urban History
Val Ginter, founder and owner
50 W. 72nd Street, New York, NY 10023
496–6859

Chicago-born Val Ginter leads scores of tours of all parts of New York City, sometimes taking a neighborhood as a subject, sometimes choosing an aspect of New York's artistic or historic life as the jumping-off point for his lecture, and sometimes combining bus rides and walks for tour groups. A former professional jazz accordionist, he leads a tour of the city's jazz history; he likes to give river-to-river tours on a single street and a Times Square theater tour, pointing out such sites as the theater where Flo Ziegfeld produced his Follies. In 1977, with Michael George, Ginter designed a tour of Grand Central Terminal, offered free to the public by the Municipal Art Society every Wednesday at 12:30 P.M. The group meets under the Kodak sign in the main concourse and covers territory from the basement level's Oyster Bar to the glass catwalks high above the terminal's concourse. Ginter still gives the tour himself often. He regularly covers all Manhattan neighborhoods—from the Wall Street historic district and South Street Seaport to Harlem—for major institutions, private groups, and the travel and tourism industry. He is the author of the book *Manhattan Trivia: The Ultimate Challenge* (Quinlan Press) and a contributor to the *New York Chronicle* (*see* **Richard McDermott**).

Joyce Gold
141 W. 17th Street, New York, NY 10011
242-5762

Ms. Gold, who holds a master's degree in metropolitan studies from New York University, where she teaches (she also teaches Manhattan history at the New School for Social Research), leads tours for major cultural institutions as well as private groups. Write to her for her annual tour schedule or for private, custom-tailored tours, given by appointment. Gold tours such neighborhoods as the financial district, Greenwich Village, Chelsea, and Ladies' Mile, (which runs from 14th Street, the northern border of Greenwich Village, up Broadway and Sixth Avenue to 23rd Street, dividing Chelsea and the Gramercy Park neighborhoods) and emphasizes history, architecture, gossip, personalities, and factual stories.

Letha Hadadi, c/o New York Open Center
83 Spring Street, New York, NY 10012
219-2527
*/**

Ms. Hadadi spent years studying acupuncture and herbology in China. Under the aegis of the center, she begins her tours with a lecture and then takes people to Chinatown's herbal medicine shops as an introduction to Chinese medicine.

Harlem Spirituals
1457 Broadway, Suite 1008, New York, NY 10036
308-2594
*/**

This firm schedules weekend trips to see Harlem by night, with dinner and a nightclub as part of the itinerary. A midweek shopping trip to 125th Street, including lunch, visits several Harlem highlights—most notably Aunt Len's Doll and Toy Museum. A Sunday morning trip features the choirs in several Harlem churches, followed by a soul-food lunch in a well-known Harlem restaurant.

Sponsoring Guides

Harlem, Your Way! Tours Unlimited, Inc.
129 W. 130th Street, New York, NY 10029
690–1687
*/**

Ms. Larcelia Kebe, the founder and president of this firm, who leads many of the walking tours herself, has created a tourism center for exploring the cultural, architectural, social, musical, and culinary highlights of Harlem. Her daily walking tour, which covers many of the historic and cultural sights of central Harlem, is described in detail in chapter 8. She will custom-tailor tours to the special needs of groups and provide a guide who will accompany a bus chartered by sightseers. She also organizes Sunday-morning church tours; brownstone walking tours; classes, given at least once a year, to instruct people in all the steps for buying brownstones; a Black History walk with a slide show and a soul-food lunch; and a nighttime club tour beginning with a champagne cocktail at her center.

Bill Harris
322 E. 18th Street, New York, NY 10003
673–1250

A former partner in Viewpoint International, a leading firm in the travel and tourism industry, Mr. Harris, a journalist and free-lance guide, conducts walking tours in Manhattan. Among his favorite neighborhoods is Murray Hill. He has written many books, including *The Plaza Hotel* (New York: Poplar Books, 1981). Tours are by appointment.

Dr. Sidney Horenstein. *See* **American Museum of Natural History.**
Inside New York
203 E. 72nd Street, New York, NY 10021
861–0709
*/**

This firm arranges tours of the art and fashion worlds for groups, with occasional do-it-yourself fashion tours on Saturdays for shoppers.

For the latter, the head of the firm meets you at an agreed-upon site on Seventh Avenue and gives you a list of designers' showrooms open to you for discount shopping on specified Saturdays.

James Kaplan, c/o Ashinoff, Ross & Goldman
747 Third Avenue, New York, NY 10017
888-7800; also, 566-0731; 765-1565; 914-834-0262
Or c/o the 92nd Street "Y."
*

Although Mr. Kaplan, a lawyer, is able to lead well-rounded tours, he has a special interest and expertise in the city's economic development from Colonial times to the present. His flagship tours, as he calls them, emphasize the development of Lower Manhattan and Brooklyn Heights. A knowledgeable economist and historian, he talks about the intertwining of politics and economics in New York's history, spinning out tales of the economic importance of the Erie Canal to the development of New York; about Brooklyn Heights as the model for the development of America's suburbs; about the entrepreneurship of Vanderbilt, Rockefeller, and other financial moguls and wizards of America; and the influence of Tammany Hall on New York and national politics.

He leads tours for some of the major cultural institutions in Manhattan and occasionally for private groups.

Jeffrey Kroessler
20-48 33rd Street, Astoria, NY 11105
718-204-8457
*

Noted as a Queens and Brooklyn specialist, Mr. Kroessler teaches history at City University of New York, specializing in the history of Queens. His neighborhood tours focus on historical and social aspects rather than on architecture. In Queens, he leads walks to Hunter's Point, Flushing, and Astoria and takes groups across the Queensboro Bridge to Long Island City. Among Brooklyn neighborhoods, his favorites are Greenpoint, Brighton Beach, Coney Island, and Atlantic Avenue on the boundary of Brooklyn Heights and Cobble Hill, which he visits either with chartered or private groups or under the auspices of the Municipal Art Society or the Queens Historical Society.

Karen Lee
787-2227
*/**

A cooking teacher and a writer of books about Chinese cuisine, Ms. Lee leads Sunday-morning tours at 9:00 A.M. on an irregular schedule for her students. These walks visit the produce stalls of Chinatown, and therefore, of course, introduce you to the enclave's lively street life and culture, giving you an insider's view of the neighborhood. The walks are open to the public.

Michael Levin
242 W. 10th Street
New York, NY 10014
924-7187

A professional historian, Chicago-born Mr. Levin has settled in Greenwich Village because of its cultural, artistic, literary, social, architectural, and natural history—all of it bountiful, eccentric, and charming in his historic-landmark district. He also leads tours of Soho, a center for New York's art scene, Wall Street, and the East Village. But the public knows him best for his 1:30 P.M. Greenwich Village tours given on Sundays, from March through early November. The walks are announced weekly in *New York Magazine* in the "Events" section. Levin also leads walks for travel firms and for special groups by appointment.

Barry Lewis
718-849-0297

Raised in Queens, Barry Lewis, an architectural historian, has served as a guide's guide and teacher for more than a decade. He currently teaches a course called "The City Transformed" under the auspices of the 92nd Street "Y." The course consists of lectures with walking tours of various city neighborhoods for city buffs and student guides. Most other professional guides have taken Lewis's course, which is open to the public on a single-ticket basis for a lecture or a walk. Lewis also does extensive tour leading for private groups and cultural institutions. Business people contemplating real-estate ventures regard him as an expert consultant.

Mr. Lewis's tours in Manhattan cover every neighborhood from the Battery to the Upper East and West Sides and Harlem, though he does not cover Murray Hill, Chelsea, or Hell's Kitchen. He is also an expert in the other boroughs, and in 1988 he undertook a course, "Neighborhoods in Transition," under the auspices of the Municipal Art Society, focusing on the outer-borough neighborhoods, with lectures and tours.

In the Bronx, the course examines the South Bronx, Mott Haven and the Hub, Morrisania and Arthur Avenue, the Fordham Road-Grand Concourse downtown area, and Parkchester. In Brooklyn, he visits Bedford-Stuyvesant, downtown Brooklyn, Clinton Hill, Crown Heights, Flatbush, Sunset Park, Bay Ridge, and Brooklyn Heights. In Queens, where he first got the notion of examining outer-borough neighborhoods, he takes groups to downtown Jamaica, Richmond Hill, Kew Gardens, Forest Hills, Jackson Heights, Sunnyside Gardens, and Long Island City. And in Staten Island, he visits the Victorian rim of the northeast section: St. George, Stapleton, and New Brighton.

Lewis also has the perfect tour-guide's voice—high-pitched and self-amplifying, to reach the outer rows of big tour groups. He's the guide with everything.

Lincoln Center
Broadway at 64th Street, New York, NY 10023
685–1800
*

Several tours visit the complex of performance spaces and libraries for the performing arts at this gracefully designed site, charming by day and spectacularly lit by night. The tours take place daily.

Sponsoring Guides

Robin Lynn
421-0109

Ms. Lynn, an architectural historian, has directed the Municipal Art Society walking-tour program in the past and has written *Walking Tours of Cast Iron Architecture in SoHo* with Margot Gayle. (Margot Gayle, though not a tour leader, was both influential and instrumental in motivating people to institute walking tours and in inspiring the current tour leaders to design and lead tours. Ms. Gayle has written books on cast-iron architecture herself as well as in collaboration with Robin Lynn.) Naturally, Soho and neighboring Tribeca are specialties for Ms. Lynn. She also gives tours of Roosevelt Island, Wall Street, Grand Central Terminal, and midtown Manhattan from Grand Central to the Seagram Building at 53rd Street and Park Avenue; she likes to do the Upper Fifth Avenue hike to see the great "châteaus."

Arthur Marks
140 E. 40th Street, New York, NY 10016
685-2761

A guide and entertainer all in one, Marks designed the walking-tour program offered by The New-York Historical Society. Marks fell in love with walking tours after going on a walk sponsored by the Museum of the City of New York under the direction of Henry Hope Reed. Marks became a Reed protégé, learning about the city and the craft of tour leading in the mid-1960s. He eventually directed the museum's program before going to The New-York Historical Society in 1987. Because he sometimes breaks into song to illustrate points on his tour lectures, imbuing his walks with especially high spirits and adding perspective as well as vitality, newspapers and magazines have written about Marks's tours quite often.

Richard McDermott
48-27 212th Street, Bayside, NY 11364
718-423-8738

Publisher of the *New York Chronicle,* a quarterly magazine about New York City, Mr. McDermott also leads tours in Manhattan, focusing on social and cultural history. His tour of Gramercy Park is delightful. In Queens he takes groups to the Alley Pond Environmental Center.

Joyce Mendelsohn
213–0481

A public-school teacher, Ms. Mendelsohn leads walking tours under the auspices of the 92nd Street "Y," which sponsors her popular Fourth of July overnight walk through the historic South Street Seaport and Wall Street areas. Entertainers, re-enacting a historic battle of the Revolutionary War, are sometimes accompanied by fife and drum players. A police escort is provided.

Metropolitan Opera Guild
1865 Broadway, New York, NY 10023
582–3512; or 582–7500
*

The guild sponsors a "Backstage at the Met" tour—a lengthy walk past the labyrinthian sets and wardrobe areas. Sometimes you can hear music wafting from the rehearsal rooms, too. And the mammoth, often fairy tale-style sets, as imaginative as gingerbread houses and as big as ships, are breathtaking.

Municipal Art Society
457 Madison Avenue, New York, NY 10022
935–3960

The M.A.S., a preservationist and educational group, has a program of regular and special tours. The Val Ginter-Michael George creation—a tour of Grand Central Terminal every Wednesday at 12:30 P.M.—is free to the public. For small fees, the M.A.S. schedules a variety of other walks, ranging from the downtown piers to the Lower East Side to Columbus Circle. Many tours support current campaigns of the M.A.S. for preservationist efforts in town.

Museum of the City of New York
Fifth Avenue at 103rd Street, New York, NY 10029
534–1672

The museum's tour program—the oldest formal program of its type in town—has been under the direction of Hope Cooke, former wife of the late ruler of Sikkim, since 1987. Some of the city's best free-lance guides have worked for and still lead tours for the museum, though the majority are given by Hope Cooke herself. Under her aegis, she says, "the museum's program traces the social history of New York City from its earliest days to its present concerns. We also try to address all present-day problems that are implicit in the whole history of the city; you don't cut off old times from now." Tours go to all the boroughs from March through May and from September through November.

Ms. Cooke brings special experience and sensibilities to the direction of the museum's program of tours, now numbering about twenty, which are aimed at presenting the social history of neighborhoods. In Sikkim, during her first marriage, she developed textbooks and curricula for Sikkimese children, to give them a perspective on their environment and the relationship of Sikkim to the rest of the world. Ms. Cooke worked in an association with the Bank Street College during her years in Sikkim, and when she returned to live in the United States, she taught Bank Street College teachers how to use the city as a laboratory for educational techniques. Ms. Cooke has a special sensitivity to her environment because she herself lived a peripatetic childhood, raised in New York City and several foreign countries. When she was married in Sikkim, she lost her U.S. citizenship and had to renew it and get a work permit on her return to her native country. So she has felt a need, which she believes she shares with immigrants in all financial circumstances, to investigate New York City.

"You can feel helpless enough in this large political morass, but if we know the city's history, then we can empower ourselves by gaining perspective on our society and our places in it," she says.

National Broadcasting Corporation
30 Rockefeller Plaza, New York, NY 10019
664–4000
*

NBC schedules several tours a day, Monday through Saturday, year-round, of the newsroom and studios of the popular daytime shows. In late November and December, there are tours on Sunday, too. You must make reservations, because "lines form around the block," as the show-biz saying goes.

New York Convention and Visitors Bureau
2 Columbus Circle, New York, NY 10019
397–8222
Also Times Square at W. 42nd Street, between Seventh Avenue and Broadway, New York, NY 10036
You will find brochures about tourist diversions in all the boroughs and an information desk at each location. Only a few walking-tour sponsors put notices of their schedules or contact numbers here, and you may have to ask at the desk at Columbus Circle to find out about them. Strictly an information service, the bureau does not sponsor tours itself.

The New-York Historical Society
170 Central Park West, New York, NY 10024
873–3400
Housed in a historic-landmark building, the society began a walking-tour series around town with **Arthur Marks** as director in 1987. The walks take place from April through early November.
The neighborhoods typically covered by the society are the Upper West Side, Astor Place, Gramercy Park, the historic Wall Street area, Greenwich Village, and Upper Fifth Avenue.

New York Stock Exchange
20 Broad Street, 3rd floor, New York, NY 10005
656–5168; and 656–3000
*
The stock exchange has an exhibit, with explanations, about the operations of the market. From a visitors' gallery, tourists can watch the action on the sprawling, paper-strewn floor. The tours take place Monday through Friday, from 9:20 A.M. to 3:30 P.M., year-round. You must check your camera at the entrance. The tour is free.

Sponsoring Guides

New York University
505–0467 for general information
Or write to School of Continuing Education, Shimkin Hall, 50 W. 4th Street, New York, NY 10003
998–7080 for general information; 998–7133 for course office.
(The courses on New York City architecture, including walking tours, are not for credit toward degrees.)
*/**
   The school sponsors several types of walking tours. Some focus on varied ethnic cuisines in town. Others concentrate on the city's architecture. **John Tauranac** and Classical America's **Michael George** teach semester-long courses on architecture with lectures and walking tours. **Rosa Ross,** a Chinese cooking-school teacher, who gives her own tours of Chinatown (*see* below), has been a guest lecturer and guide for N.Y.U. Experts on archaeology and theater lead tours of museums and theatrical performances. Still other tour/class combinations take you to Lincoln Center for the Performing Arts to see ballet, opera, theater, and concerts. Courses, subjects, and teacher-leaders are subject to change every semester.

New York Walkabout, c/o Lister Travel Service
30 Rockefeller Plaza, New York, NY 10019
582–2015; or 582–3460
   This private firm schedules walks in many areas of New York City, from the "Gold Coast" of the Fifth Avenue mansions to Greenwich Village, Brooklyn Heights, the Lower East Side, and many points in between and beyond. Each season has its own schedule of tours; most walks take place first thing in the morning and are repeated in the afternoon.

The 92nd Street YMHA/YWHA
Lexington Avenue at 92nd Street, New York, NY 10128
427–6000
   The "Y" has the most extensive tour program in town, with walks ranging from a couple of hours to all-day trips, to lengthy vacations,

some of them to foreign countries. Most of the best free-lance guides give one or several tours per year for the "Y." In addition to neighborhood walks, with many different approaches to some neighborhoods, the "Y" sponsors tours with themes to visit the art world or other cultural scenes. Tours take place year-round.

Everett Ortner
718–638–3128
*/**

With his wife, Evelyn, Mr. Ortner leads tours of Brooklyn brownstones by private appointment. He is chairman of the Brownstone Revival Committee of New York and is therefore called upon to take busloads of people on tours designed for large groups, beginning in Manhattan neighborhoods and traveling to Brooklyn. At the various brownstone sites, Mr. Ortner takes the groups on little walks. Usually the tours end with lunch at the Montauk Club, a restaurant housed in a nineteenth-century, Venetian Gothic landmark building, which has stood for 100 years in Park Slope, Brooklyn.

Park Rangers
397–3080, for information about tours in Central Park and other Manhattan parks. The office can also refer you to Park Rangers who lead walks in other boroughs for their schedules. In Brooklyn, for Prospect Park, call 718–287–5252.
*

The Park Rangers lead free tours every weekend in Central Park, focusing on different aspects of history, bird, plant, and animal life, and the weather. The Rangers are quite versatile: they can even teach photographic techniques for nature shots. Occasionally they lead walks through some of the smaller parks, and on holidays they schedule special events, such as a Halloween tour for kids in Washington Square Park in Greenwich Village. The repertoire of tours in the various parks changes, so call for up-to-date information.

In summer, Manhattan's Inwood Park usually activates a substation of the Park Rangers and conducts regular tours. Ranger bases are located in the following big parks in the other boroughs, and Rangers there conduct regular tours or can refer you to special walks:

Bronx: Crotona Park, 589–0096; Van Cortlandt Park, 548–7880

Queens: Flushing Meadow Park, 718–699–4204

Staten Island: Silver Lakes Park, 718–816–5456.

Also, the Park Rangers Directors compile a tour schedule. Call one to two months in advance of the day you wish to tour, if you want a written brochure mailed to you. The address is: Park Rangers Directors, 1234 Fifth Avenue, New York, NY 10029.

Prospect Park Environmental Center
Tennis House, Prospect Park, Brooklyn, NY 11215
718–788–8500
*/**

For a recorded announcement of the week's programs, call 718–788–8544

Founded in 1978 by John Muir, an urban geographer, the center sponsors about forty tours a year, in all seasons, primarily in Brooklyn's Prospect Park and urban neighborhoods. Walks range from the Brooklyn Bridge to Greenwood Cemetery, Coney Island's subway yards, construction sites, and the railroad tunnel under Atlantic Avenue. Some tours take place on foot, others by boat or bus. Some are workshop tours for photography instruction, gravestone rubbing, and other educational activities. The P.P.E.C. sometimes cosponsors tours with other groups such as the Municipal Art Society.

Queens Historical Society
143–35 37th Avenue, Flushing, NY 11354
718–939–0647
*

The society sponsors approximately ten to fifteen tours a year, mostly between March and November. Several Queens residents lead tours of the borough's neighborhoods; among the guides are **Barry Lewis; Jeffrey Kroessler;** Vincent Seyfried, a vice-president of the

Queens Historical Society and a local historian; Dr. Jack Eichenbaum, an urban geographer; and Robert Miller, a film technician in the Queens Borough Public Library who leads a tour of the Long Island Motor Parkway, the first parkway to be built for cars.

Radio City Music Hall
50th Street at Sixth Avenue, New York, NY 10019
246–4600, ext. 263
*

The great art deco theater schedules tours of its interior several times a day.

Henry Hope Reed
753–4376
also c/o Classical America
Mr. Reed has written books on the grandeur of classical architecture and classical principles in all the arts; he also founded the walking-tour movement in New York City in 1955. (*See* the sketch of Classical America.) Mr. Reed does not lead tours himself, but his protégé, **Michael George,** takes charge of about ten tours a year for the group.

Rosa Ross
777–3420
*/**

A teacher of Chinese culinary arts, Ms. Ross leads irregularly scheduled walks in Chinatown, visiting shops and produce stalls, peppering her lectures with insights into Chinese culture. She takes her groups, primarily students, for a dim sum lunch as part of the produce tour. The walks are open to the public.

Pete Salwen
873–1944
*

Mr. Salwen, who is writing a book about New York City's Upper West Side, is best known to the public as the leader of an annual Mark

Sponsoring Guides

Twain tour given during the last weekend in November. Salwen traces the history of Twain's career in Greenwich Village, from his arrival as a teenager in town, through his return to New York as an admired journalist and raconteur.

Schapiro's Winery
126 Rivington Street, New York, NY 10002
475-7383
*

In what was once the heart of New York City's bustling Jewish neighborhood of immigrants from Eastern Europe, this winery—Manhattan's only one—produces all styles and forms of kosher wine in a dank cellar. It's open to the pubic free of charge on Sundays. It's also suggested that you buy a bottle of wine, which can cost as little as $2. Other, longer tours of the Lower East Side make the winery one of their stops.

Joseph L. Schiff
50 W. 72nd Street, New York, NY 10023
362-0365
*/**

Mr. Schiff specializes in "Jewish Urban Study Tours," and his firm may be listed as JUST in the phone book by the time you read this book; if not, call him at the above number under his own name. His premise is that a Jewish education exists in the neighborhoods where Jews have left their stamp on the city's history, culture, and religion. Schiff's tours explore the many Hasidic groups living together in Borough Park, Brooklyn; the traces of early (seventeenth-century) Jewish settlers in Lower Manhattan; the Lower East Side "World of Our Fathers," which had its heyday from 1880 to 1920; Brooklyn's Hasidic Satmar group in Williamsburg; Crown Heights; and Manhattan's Upper West Side, where "Marjorie Morningstar," the fictional heroine of Herman Wouk's novel of the same name, was raised surrounded by prospering Jewish families. Schiff also goes to Washington Heights and Yeshiva University; the Jewish Theological Seminary at Broadway and 122nd Street (where Schiff studied); and Hebrew Union College in Greenwich Village, for a look at the Orthodox, Conservative, and Reform Rabbinical seminaries.

Professor James Shenton
Columbia University, Room 324, New York, NY 10027
280–1754; and 280–4532

Dr. Shenton, a history professor, gives highly regarded tours of New York City, both on Columbia's campus and in many neighborhoods, on an irregular schedule.

Professor Shenton's tours cover Harlem; Arthur Avenue, in an Italian neighborhood in the Bronx; Brighton Beach and Brooklyn Heights in Brooklyn; Chinatown, Little Italy, and the former Irish New York; Greek Astoria in Queens; Columbia University and Morningside Heights; the Upper West Side; and Greenwich Village.

Since Dr. Shenton is in his university office on an irregular schedule, you may also contact him through a university administration number, 280–2838; ask for Mr. Joe Kissone.

Jeff Sholeen
718–522–4162

Mr. Sholeen leads tours for various cultural groups. He began in the early 1980s with the Museum of the City of New York, and since then has also guided walks for the American Institute of Architects (A.I.A.), the American Bibliographical Society, the Victorian Society in America—Metropolitan Chapter, and for out-of-towners and others visiting museums. He is noted for his expertise on the Victorian and modern periods. Now an employee at an art gallery specializing in Georgian furniture, he majored in architectural history at the University of Illinois and is a candidate for an M.S. degree in the Historic Preservation Program at Columbia University. The degree combines architectural history, city planning, restoration techniques, and preservation law.

Singer's Tours
130 St. Edwards Street, Brooklyn, NY 11201
718–875–9084
*/**

Lou Singer leads tours of brownstones in Brooklyn neighborhoods, many in close proximity to Manhattan, and also schedules walks through the Lower East Side and parts of Greenwich Village in Manhattan for highlights of Jewish history, culture, and religion; and multi-ethnic food tasting, including Italian, Chinese, and Eastern European cuisines.

Shore Walkers of New York
Cy Adler, founder and leader
241 E. 97th Street, New York, NY 10025
663-2167
*

This firm schedules short (five miles is considered short for this group) tours of the city's shorelines, sometimes crossing bridges and touching three boroughs in one day. The group has actually circumnavigated Manhattan and walked from the source of the Hudson River down to Manhattan. That tour gets press coverage, of course.

Sidewalks of New York
517-0201
This firm opened on December 1, 1987, to lead neighborhood and novelty or theme tours in Manhattan. Among the neighborhoods covered by the firm's six staff guides by the summer of 1988 were Gramercy Park and Greenwich Village. There are also tours of sites in town where films have been made and of movie stars' houses; and a tavern tour that takes people to McSorley's on E. 7th Street, the Lion's Head, Chumley's, the White Horse Tavern, where Dylan Thomas became a legendary drinker, the Minetta Tavern, and the Grand Ticino. Other themes for tours are famous murder sites and rock-and-roll landmarks.

The firm's founder, Sam Stafford, suggests that you make reservations. However, if you decide to call the firm and go on one of the tours listed on its answering machine on the same day it's given, just go to the starting place at the proper time. Tours are also announced in advance in many periodicals and newspapers circulating primarily in New York City. These include *New York* Magazine, *7 Days, New York Almanac, On the Avenue, New York Press,* the *West Side Spirit, Our Town,* and the Friday editions of the *Daily News,* the *New York Post,* and sometimes the *New York Times.*

Ron Spence
368–1876
*

Mr. Spence, a lifetime resident of Harlem, is the sole guide for a firm called Harlem Renaissance, and he occasionally leads tours of Harlem's various neighborhoods, starting in Morningside Heights, for that firm and for schools and cultural institutions. His tours include such high-lights as the view from the Bell Tower of Riverside Church and a walk through Harlem's Sugar Hill area.

Staten Island Historical Society
Education Department, 441 Clarke Avenue, Staten Island, NY 10306
718–351–9414
*

The society sponsors a few tours every year, which are led by the society's curators and restoration staffers. Richmondtown, which used to be the borough's county seat, is always on the list, with its 1837 court-house, twenty-five other historic buildings, and historic sites, including battlefields in the area.

Sutton Area Community, Inc.
SAC—Box A, 60 Sutton Place, New York, NY 10022
*

An exceptionally community-minded group, representing a small, very wealthy enclave on the Upper East Side, the SAC sponsors tours and other projects to keep this neighborhood elite and conscious of its status.

John Tauranac
878–7023; and 222–7731
A consultant with the Metropolitan Transportation Authority, this professional guide, an adjunct assistant professor of arts who lectures about New York City's architecture in a noncredit course at New York University's School of Continuing Education, is also a writer. He has published two books about New York: *Essential New York* (Holt Rine-

hart and Winston) and *Elegant New York, 1885–1915, The Builders, The Buildings* (Abbeville Press). He developed the M.T.A.'s subway, bus, and neighborhood maps for New York City, and in 1988 he designed museum maps for the five boroughs. An architectural historian, he says his interest lies primarily in the physical city. "Give me God's concrete, not God's country," he sums up.

A native New Yorker whose father worked for a fashionable hotel and constantly talked about the city's physical attributes, Tauranac gives tours of many neighborhoods, among them City Hall to the Battery along Broadway; the Upper West Side from Columbus Circle to the Apthorp Apartments; the subways; the Gold Coast from the Carnegie House (now the Cooper-Hewitt Museum) at 91st Street and Fifth Avenue to the Rhinelander House at 72nd Street and Madison Avenue; Gramercy Park with charming nineteenth-century architecture and a private park; The Cathedral Church of St. John The Divine on Morningside Heights to Grant's Tomb; and the East Village, in the area of Cooper Union.

Mr. Tauranac does free-lance tours for groups and also leads groups for the Municipal Art Society, the 92nd Street "Y," the National Fine Arts Associates, and others.

Viewpoint International
1414 Avenue of the Americas, New York, NY 10019
355-1055
*/**

The office is open from 9:30 A.M. to 5:30 P.M. on weekdays, but the switchboard is open twenty-four hours a day, seven days a week. The company designs high-priced tours for small groups, offering transportation by bus to sites where people get out, walk around, and look. There's a historic tour of Greenwich Village; an art tour of the Soho galleries, where tourists meet with artists; bargain shopping on the Lower East Side; an antiques tour; a visit to historic houses in many neighborhoods; a food tour; and a design/decoration tour. The firm also leads excursions to the Hudson Valley and to Long Island's Gold Coast.

This company packages tours for conventions and is one of about eighty-five companies in New York City offering such a service. Others are Red Carpet, Passkey, Briggs Convention Associates, and Convention Tours Unlimited. The tours offered by these firms are custom-tailored and so various that they can include ball games and zoos as well as neighborhoods. The firms hire such guides as **Val Ginter** and **Michael Levin.**

Gerard Wolfe
777–4747

An experienced and popular guide to Manhattan neighborhoods, Dr. Wolfe is a professor of Romance Languages at New York University and occasionally teaches courses about architectural history in the School of Continuing Education there. He's the author of *New York: A Guide to the Metropolis,* reissued as a McGraw-Hill paperback in 1988, and an older book, *The Synagogues of New York's Lower East Side* (N.Y. University Press, 1977). He gives tours throughout the tristate area; in Manhattan, as a generalist for the 92nd Street "Y," the New York Council for the Humanities, and the Smithsonian Institution, he has several favorite neighborhoods. Among them are Ladies' Mile (between Chelsea and Gramercy Park), Greenwich Village, Lower Manhattan (for its history and architecture), and Brooklyn Heights.

Joe Zito
581–9384

A retired New York City police captain who has habitually, out of intellectual curiosity, visited other cities and walked their lengths and breadths on vacations, Joe Zito leads tours in Manhattan and Brooklyn neighborhoods as a free-lancer and for major cultural and educational institutions. Of all the neighborhoods, he prefers Hell's Kitchen, an area of Manhattan with old connections to politics and crime, on the fringes of the theater district, beginning at Eighth Avenue in the West Fifties and running all the way to the Hudson River. Zito also does a tour of the Tenderloin. This is the area below Hell's Kitchen, in the West Thirties,

Sponsoring Guides

now dominated by Macy's, Madison Square Garden, and Herald Center, but once a juicy, seamy area for the crooked. Mr. Zito leads tours from April through November.

Chapter Three

Greenwich Village

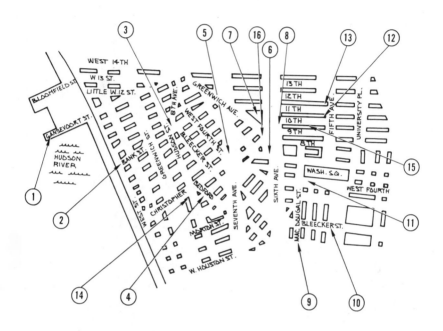

Points of Interest in Greenwich Village and the West Side

1. Gansevoort Street pier
2. Bank Street
3. Abdingdon Square
4. Bedford Street
5. Sheridan Square
6. Gay Street
7. Patchin Place
8. Milligan Place
9. Macdougal Street

10. Bleecker Street
11. Washington Square
12. Ascension Episcopal Church
13. First Presbyterian Church
14. St. Luke's in the Fields
15. Mark Twain's Greenwich-Village House
16. Jefferson Market Courthouse

Of all the neighborhoods in New York City, Greenwich Village reigns as the most popular. Here's a profile of the neighborhood, with highlights of several excellent tours and a list of the guides who often lead them.

Every generalist among the professional guides has at least one excellent walking tour of Greenwich Village in his or her repertoire. The architecture of this charming district makes it a magnet. New Yorkers from other neighborhoods and boroughs come in droves to the Village for weekend-afternoon outings, especially to browse in the organized art festival in late May and early June and again in late August and early September. Often people simply arrive to have dinner in their favorite, romantic old bistros. Many of these last for decades, while new ones arrive to replace those that linger only a few years; all of them keep alive the Village's reputation for style and good, multi-ethnic cuisines, sometimes still at economical prices.

Out-of-towners usually choose the Village walking tours over all the others, because the Village retains the mystique it began to acquire near the beginning of the century—and, even before. In the late nineteenth and early twentieth centuries, bohemians, writers, and other artists moved into the neighborhood's affordable "French flats," so named because the middle class, who lived in private family houses, viewed any living arrangement with bedrooms right next to the living rooms as too sexy and risqué—certain to lead to the destruction of traditional family units and values. In short, these apartments were too "French" in spirit.

Nevertheless, apartment living was practical. Such luminaries as Eugene O'Neill, Edna St. Vincent Millay, and e. e. cummings found affordable apartments here, and helped to give the area its quirky cachet. Though other neighborhoods have become more trendy and glamorous, many out-of-towners still know almost nothing about New York City except for the legendary quaintness of Greenwich Village and its reputation as a haven for intellectuals, painters, writers, mavericks, revolutionaries, and sexual individualists. It is for this reason that cultural institutions always include at least one and usually several Village tours in any year's fare, and every professional guide offers at least one Village tour.

The undying allure of the Village, with its charming, one- and two-century-old buildings on a human scale—usually three or four stories high—overrides the changing fashions and fortunes of the rest of town. People can always conjure up an image of attractive, careless youngsters dining in candle-lit bistros, chatting about Woody Allen's life-view. Those in the know may have even spotted Allen at his favorite pizzeria, John's, on Bleecker Street. Even though the type of people many associate with the Village have, for the most part, actually settled in other, more affordable—or in some cases more expensive—neighborhoods, the Village still supports its reputation as an exotic haven for the country's most creative, pace-setting, and free-spirited personalities. And of course some remain.

By the late eighteenth century, the Village began building its reputation as a melting pot for great and vivid minds and sensual bodies. Tom Paine, the author of *Common Sense,* lived here even earlier. He died impoverished and maligned, because of his atheism and despite his great patriotism. But he did call the Village home for a while. A hundred years later, dapper Mark Twain, a Village resident, also beset by personal troubles, made his home here for many years.

Soon after the turn of the century, Eugene O'Neill and other struggling writers moved in. Journalist John Reed repaired to a table in a popular village café and wrote *Ten Days That Shook the World.* He did this in public for the simple reason that he couldn't find space to work in his tiny apartment in a mews, a former stable, which he shared with his lover (eventually his wife), Louise Bryant. She also became O'Neill's lover. They belonged to a crowd that coaxed O'Neill out of a bar and locked him up to write *The Emperor Jones,* which established the Provincetown Playhouse as a power in the theater world.

Edna St. Vincent Millay burned her candle at both ends, as an impassioned poetess and a legendary lover in the Village, as Michael Levin, an eminent professional guide to the Village, tells his walking-tour groups nowadays. In her Village period, Millay added fuel to the fire of the neighborhood's reputation.

By mid-twentieth century, Villagers busied themselves with attaining historical-landmark status for the neighborhood, protecting it from demolition. Real estate values climbed. Some artists, writers, and musicians with rent-controlled apartments lingered on. And wealthy actors came to buy entire houses, which nowadays can cost between $2 and $5 million.

The Village's tranquil, manicured buildings puzzle visitors who hope to stumble upon a wild party in the streets. Indeed, the visitors themselves cause most of the public commotion. On weekend days, particularly in spring, summer, and fall, you can see groups ranging in size from baseball teams to overcrowded classrooms trailing tour leaders through the narrow streets. Some of them zigzag, following the old borders of long-gone farms. Popular tour leaders have developed resounding voices, especially handy for shouting in the Village streets: "Stay out of the street! Cars come whizzing through here!" And one seasoned leader, Arthur Marks, even jumps on a stoop and sings raucously: "Come a little closer, love be mine!" to cajole people onto the sidewalk.

Justin Ferate, a Brooklyn specialist, can lead tours of the Village's historic buildings and add some offbeat fillips that other tour leaders don't include: for example, the collection of Fabergé eggs, military exhibit pieces, toy boats, and the bill in pounds sent by Paul Revere to the Continental Congress for his historic ride—all within the Forbes Building's ground-floor collection, 60 Fifth Avenue at 12th Street.

Val Ginter, a native of Chicago, who fell in love with his father's collection of New York stereographs as a child, has his own firm, Ginter-Gotham Urban History, established by word of mouth as a leading firm. And though he has worked for all the major cultural institutions in the city, Ginter does the majority of his tours for private clients these days. Like many of the best guides, Ginter is versatile. For example, he can lead a tour from the Hudson to the East rivers, on 14th Street, the Village's northern border: "It's a great urban kaleidoscope," he says, "from the meat market and Chelsea piers, where the Titanic would have arrived, and the Lusitania used to come in." The tour proceeds through Little Spain (an area between Seventh and Eighth avenues, primarily), where you can still see Spanish businesses, goes past the new, glamorous Zeckendorf Towers at Union Square, skirts the border of the old Yiddish theater territory, and winds up at the former gashouse district.

Since 14th Street divides the West Village from Chelsea and Ladies' Mile, the route allows Ginter, at several avenues, to point uptown and show tourists the massive buildings on Sixth Avenue and Broadway that once housed many of New York's department stores.

The earnest-mannered Ginter, who gets up at 4:00 A.M. to polish his lectures on tour days, sometimes leads an all-day tour of the East and West Villages—"the ultimate tour," he calls it. It begins near the junction of 14th Street and Second Avenue, an area that once constituted the heart of the German community in New York City. But following the General Slocum disaster, in which the wives and children of many German residents drowned while riding on a weekend pleasure-boat trip, the German widowers moved en masse to other neighborhoods, trying to erase the scene of their past joys and their tragic loss from their memories. Soon the immigrant Jews from Eastern Europe moved to this neighborhood from the Lower East Side, replacing the German community and establishing theaters and many other businesses.

In the West Village, for out-of-towners who have never seen the area, Ginter is likely to concentrate on the confusing warren of streets, where, for example, W. 11th crosses W. 4th. He explains that the streets once constituted the borders of farmlands. He also points out highlights, including the 1799 Isaac-Hendricks house at 77 Bedford Street, the Village's oldest house, hard by the narrowest one (only $9^{1}/_2$ feet wide) at

75¹/₂ Bedford Street where Edna St. Vincent Millay and John Barrymore, Sr., among other celebrities, lived at different times.

Joyce Gold, a teacher at the New School, a writer, and a tour guide,
leads tours by reservations made directly with her. Among her four
favorite areas is Greenwich Village. Instead of concentrating on the
nineteenth century, as so many guides to the Village do, Ms.
Gold goes back to the eighteenth century, tracing the route of the Minetta Water, a
legendary, and some even say mythical, stream that used to separate
Greenwich Village from the rest of Manhattan. It was supposedly filled
in between 1790 and 1810. On her tour, she also tries to teach people to
differentiate between quaint buildings that date back, for example, to
1810 and others that were built in 1850, by pointing out clues in the
brickwork and the roof constructions.

Beginning at Washington Square, once a cemetery for thousands of
people, she makes her way around New York University's campus, talking about the land as it existed several hundred years ago. She progresses to Sixth Avenue, during a three-to-four-hour tour, settles people
down for a cappuccino, and then leads them to the Hudson River, looking for traces of the Village in its early stages of development. Some
people believe that the Village in the early nineteenth century served as
a haven for refugees from the epidemics at the lower end of Manhattan.
In any case, the Village had healthy, country air and developed first as
farmland outside the city proper. The streets today follow the outlines of
the old farm boundaries. Ms. Gold's tour ends at the Jefferson Market
Courthouse, now a branch of the New York Public Library and a historic
landmark in several architectural styles.

Michael Levin, of all the guides, is the best-known Village specialist.
Chicago-born, with two graduate degrees in history, Levin regularly ad-
vertises his Sunday tours, from March through November, in *New York*
magazine. He also offers custom-tailored tours during the rest of the
week for groups by appointment. He once led a New Year's Eve party
tour, and, when the walk ended, watched his group get into taxis and go
to toast the New Year in the host's apartment.

Greenwich Village

For information about his Sunday-afternoon tours, which begin at about 1:30 P.M. and last ninety minutes—watch the magazine announcements—he offers a variety of routes and topics. One day he retraces the footsteps of the Village writers, artists, mavericks, and revolutionaries in the bohemian days. He tells ghost stories indigenous to the Village on the Sunday closest to Halloween. Another day he recounts the history of the East Village from the days of Dutch Governor Peter Stuyvesant to those of pop-art guru Andy Warhol. Occasionally he visits the West Village's harbor.

Here's a taste of his "Bohemian Days" tour. Levin stops for about twenty minutes on winding, narrow Gay Street, pointing out the houses that were once owned by Mayor Jimmy Walker, and reminisces about Walker's adulterous affair with actress Betty Compton, whom he later married. She lived in a house he owned on Gay Street and he often stayed with her before his divorce. (He and his wife were living in a nearby street just across Seventh Avenue.) Levin proceeds down Gay Street, where Ruth McKenney, the author of *My Sister Eileen,* did indeed live with her sister, to another house on Waverly Place, around the corner from Gay Street, where Edna St. Vincent Millay carried on the kind of love life that made the Village a renowned haven for anyone looking for an unfettered life-style. One finds out from Levin that Millay was named for St. Vincent's Hospital in the Village.

Her mother's brother was an alcoholic who had the temerity to fall asleep aboard a ship anchored in New Orleans. By the time the crew discovered him, he was bound for New York City. The crew deposited him in St. Vincent's Hospital, because he was quite ill. When his sister heard about his good fortune, she promised to name her child, with whom she was pregnant, in honor of his recovery, for which she was praying. The baby was Edna St. Vincent Millay, who always felt a particular attraction to the neighborhood.

Levin spouts engaging tales of other Village standard-setters. At the junction of Greenwich Avenue, Sixth Avenue, Eighth Street, and Ninth Street, for example, he points out the area where Luke O'Connor's Columbian Tavern was located from 1893 to the 1920s. Known as the Working Girls' House, it was one of the few bars where a woman could enter unescorted and not be mistaken for a prostitute. A local school-teacher who frequented this bar also flouted convention by marrying, in the days when it was illegal for a schoolteacher to marry in New York and many other states. She went without a corset, bobbed her hair, and wore ballet slippers, generally inventing the bohemian style that came to be known as the "Village look." It had a nationwide vogue during the folksong craze of the 1950s and '60s.

Barry Lewis, the teaching guide who has inspired so many city buffs, has several favorite tours of the Village. For one, he starts at Washington Square, concentrating on the architecture and artifacts of the area, and then leads his groups up Fifth Avenue and through the streets from 8th through 13th between Fifth and Sixth avenues—streets filled with mes-merizingly beautiful old landmark buildings—"the real Village," as Mr. Lewis says. At the corner of 9th Street and Sixth Avenue, he pauses at the former Jefferson Market Courthouse and talks about its hybrid archi-tectural style and its symbolism as a one-time civic center and a contin-uing spiritual beacon for Village residents. Once it was targeted for demolition, but Villagers rallied and saved it. The also managed to bring about the landmark designation of the entire Village. From there, Mr. Lewis usually proceeds further west, via Christopher Street, to the "Far West" Village—once considered the downside of the neighborhood in terms of social standing and architecture. The Far West Village, how-ever, has many quaint buildings of artistic note, all of which, being well kept and tended, afford tourists glimpses of a memorable past. The tours usually end at Hudson Street.

Another Lewis favorite starts at the eastern border of the Village—Cooper Union, founded by Peter Cooper in the nineteenth century to offer free education for all and dedicated to the advancement of science and art. From Cooper Square, Mr. Lewis walks downtown, onto Lafay-ette Street, which was once midtown Manhattan and one of the most fashionable neighborhoods in which to live in the early to mid-nineteenth century. For decades, it fell into disrepair, neglected, as soci-ety residents pushed uptown. But then Joseph Papp took over a building scheduled for demolition. It had been the first public library in New

York, built with Astor money in the mid-nineteenth century. Papp turned it into the Public Theater, a venerable cultural institution with many performance spaces. Mr. Papp's theater has given birth to new, important playwrights, actors, and other theater artists. It has also helped glamorize the neighborhood, attracting artists and theater people to move in and open performance spaces and art galleries. Phebe's Place, a neighborhood bar and restaurant, is known as a hangout for theater people. The Lewis tour takes a look at some of the historic-landmark buildings for their architectural charms and proceeds west, to Washington Square, winding up at the former Jefferson Market Courthouse.

Arthur Marks, a New York City guide for twenty years, designed a series of tours for The New-York Historical Society in 1987, calling his Village tour "Scholars and Sybarites." It was so popular in its first year that he needed seven assistants to lead supplementary groups on the Sunday-afternoon walk.

With the breezy, outgoing style of a seasoned performer, Marks, on one of his tours, burst into song at several sites, singing Broadway tunes from plays about Mayor Fiorello La Guardia and his corrupt predecessor, Gentleman Jimmy Walker. Both were born in the Village. Writer Ruth McKenney and her sister Eileen got their song renditions, too.

Marks's song about Walker underscored the former Mayor's explanation to investigators that he quit smoking for a week and put the money he saved in a little tin box. It financed wondrous things, Mark's raspy voice resounded. In between his songs, which at least shed light on Broadway's and the media's view of the quality of historic hijinx in the Village, he disseminated information about the neighborhood and its residents with witticisms and ironic insights.

He pointed out the site of the Triangle Shirtwaist Factory fire, near Henry James's birthplace (slightly east of Washington Square) and explained the purpose behind such minute details as the boot scrapers on wrough-iron balustrades outside West Village townhouses: "The roads were unpaved and muddy; pigs and dogs roamed around." Wending his way from Washington Square toward the Hudson for two hours—"at the end, we'll all jump into the Hudson," he cracked—sporting an elegant

Italian felt hat with a wide brim, he reconstructed the Village's history. He had arranged for his group to visit a (usually) locked private garden called Grove Court, originally built for workers who constructed the Village's loftier residences. Nowadays, Grove Court, with an island of ivy at the entranceway, and a bright yellow covering of yellow gingko-tree leaves in the fall, constitutes an enclave of the wealthy, the well-connected, and lucky old leaseholders. Marks pointed out the differences between Queen Anne-Revival-style and Federalist-style roofs in the neighborhood, for those who like their quaintness analyzed.

A New-York Historical Society tour always ends with a reception; in the Village, the society provided cookies, cake, and coffee in a building belonging to St. Luke's in the Fields, a historic Episcopal church on Hudson Street.

The Museum of the City of New York sponsors an East and West Village tour combined, called "Society Separates: the East and West Villages." According to the museum's brochure, "a flight from yellow fever sparked the development of the West Village as a gentry boom-town in the 1820s, while bloody class riots at the Astor Place Opera House in the 1840s spurred the gentry's flight and the subsequent immigrant settlement in that community." The museum tour visits the two villages and discusses their separate heritages.

The West Village was farm country at the end of the seventeenth century and for part of the eighteenth century. Stagecoaches stopped in the Village territory on their way north, and there was a ferry stop here from New Jersey. The Village was a pleasant, idyllic place, ideal for a day in the country. Epidemics of cholera, typhoid, and typhus led people to go to the Village, looking for cleaner air. In summer, the Village made an ideal vacation spot. Eventually, as the city grew and New Yorkers sought more space, the Village became an attractive place to live.

Halfway across the island, near where Cooper Union stands, Lafayette Street was a prestigious address in the 1800s. (According to Dr. James Shenton, a historian at Columbia University, the riots in the Astor Place theater were caused by the Irish, who got themselves involved in the question of whether an Irishman or an Englishman should play "Hamlet" there in 1849.)

Greenwich Village

Beginning in 1840 and continuing into the 1870s, New York City's population tripled to 900,000, and Greenwich Village was affected by this growth. The new settlers were primarily working-class people in search of inexpensive housing. By the mid-1870s literary people looking for affordable housing began to settle in the Village. It gradually became a more prestigious place to live—and a mélange, which it remains, to some extent, to this day. At the same time, the East Village became a popular settlement for ethnic immigrant groups, as they pushed their way uptown, trying to integrate into American society and establish themselves financially.

New York Walkabout, in the same office as the Lister Travel Service, conducts several tours of the Village every year. Some explore the West Village's winding streets—the Village of the bohemians and theater people, including O'Neill and Barrymore; and the Washington Square Park area. Another tour visits Astor Place and the East Village. The neighborhood, once a very fashionable place to live, now is home to Cooper Union and the Public Theater.

Pete Salwen conducts his "Mark Twain Anniversary Tour" on the last weekend in November to memorialize the anniversary of Mark Twain's birthday in 1835. Salwen, who was born in New York City, raised for a while in New Jersey, and then brought back to the city to finish growing up, fell in love with Mark Twain memorabilia brought home by his father. Pete became a city buff, and decided to design a Mark Twain tour to honor the writer's 150th birthday anniversary. The walk has become an annual fixture, usually under the auspices of the Mark Twain Association.

The three-hour tour begins a few blocks south of Houston Street, on Broadway, near Spring Street, where Twain lived as an impoverished teenager in his first days in town. He left to become a foreign correspondent; when he returned, he was quite well-known. Salwen proceeds uptown, cutting across Houston to Lafayette Street, stopping at the sites where Twain used to go drinking in popular bars of the day and telling anecdotes about Twain's gregariousness. Salwen makes his way to Gramercy Park, where, along with the Shakespearean actor Edwin Booth and others, Twain helped to found the Players Club. Though Twain is remembered as a writer, he was at least as well-known in his era for storytelling and lecturing; his pace of delivery was slow, and his timing was the envy of many performers.

Twain also started a publishing company on Union Square at 14th Street, to which Salwen meanders from Gramercy Park. The tour ends at a Greenwich Village brownstone just west of Fifth Avenue, where Twain lived. He was a familiar, dapper sight, walking down Fifth Avenue in a bright white suit, as his friends and neighbors were emerging from church on Sunday mornings in proper black. Salwen pops a cork from a champagne bottle and shares the bubbly with sightseers on his tour.

Professor James Shenton's tour emphasizes the Village's role as a suburb in the latter part of the nineteenth century, when intellectuals and writers were attracted by the area's cheap rents and pleasant ambience. Dr. Shenton discusses some of the intellectuals and writers who lived, and in some cases died, here: Tom Paine, Edna St. Vincent Millay, Willa Cather, and Washington Irving.

Chapter Four

Soho, Tribeca, Upper East Side, and Wall Street

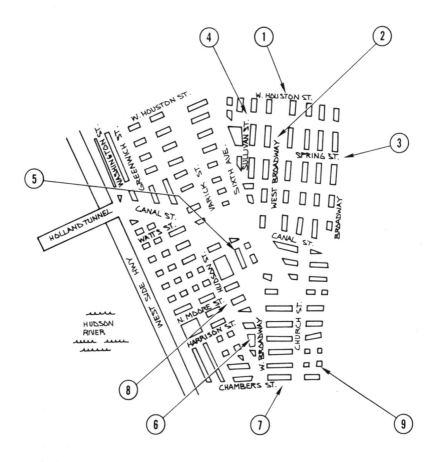

Points of Interest in Soho and Tribeca

1. West Houston Street
2. West Broadway
3. Spring Street
4. Sullivan Street
5. American Thread Building
6. Western Union Building
7. Chambers Street
8. Hudson Street area
9. Sun Building

After Greenwich Village, one of the most popular tours in town goes to Soho, the artists' district, just below the Village, and sometimes ventures into Tribeca, an adjacent art gallery district. When the Village became a historic-landmark district in the middle of the twentieth century, rents climbed so high that artists couldn't afford the spaces. They effected a virtual "brain drain" into the community to the south, bounded by Houston Street on the north (hence the acronym *Soho* for *So*uth of *Ho*uston Street). Eventually this loft district, where gifted artists renovated disintegrating, abandoned industrial spaces of cavernous dimensions in cast-iron buildings, became so expensive that the artists themselves were "priced out" of the neighborhood and forced to look once again for spaces at lower rents elsewhere. At first they turned their attention to Tribeca (the *Tri*angle *be*low *Ca*nal Street), another district of cast-iron buildings. No sooner had the artists started to salvage them than the real estate speculators turned the district into another fashionable quarter for residences and restaurants. So the galleries never migrated to Tribeca in considerable numbers. For sight-seeing, however, Soho and Tribeca have magical visual attributes that anyone can afford on a walking tour.

Also very popular is the Upper East Side, nicknamed the "Gold Coast." Tours usually stake out small sections of the area to give sightseers a tasteful slice of the good life that suggests the entire quality of the area from St. Patrick's Cathedral to the East 90s.

Wall Street's historic district, the oldest in town, is also popular. It sprawls from City Hall and the courts in the Civic Center down to the Battery and east to the South Street Seaport. Because these highlights are at a considerable distance from each other, tours sometimes cover only part of the territory.

Soho and Tribeca

These neighborhoods are renowned for their massive art galleries coexisting with trendy restaurants and boutiques, which offer indescribable concoctions to eat and wear at astronomical prices. Since the late 1960s, first Soho, then Tribeca (since the late '70s), have undergone a renaissance.

Soho's cast-iron buildings, erected in the period between 1850 and World War I, when cast iron was a fashionable building material, were originally zoned for industrial tenants only. By the late 1960s, landlords closed their eyes to artists who moved into the lofts abandoned by industry and reclaimed them for full-time illegal living as well as legal working spaces. Artists did such remarkable renovation jobs that they turned the cast-iron district into a desirable neighborhood. The artists also lobbied until the city declared the neighborhood legal for living and gave it a landmark designation to protect it from demolition. Then the artists turned their sights on Tribeca, where similar activity began.

Speculators, developers, entertainers, and "beautiful people" moved into Tribeca right away, sending prices soaring above the means of the artists. So they moved again—to Hoboken, New Jersey, Chelsea, Long Island City, and especially to the East Village, with its lively gallery scene. Tribeca's restaurants have become more fashionable for denizens of the art world than Soho's and also attract diners from the government and Wall Street financial offices, particularly at lunchtime.

Most tours of Soho and Tribeca include their history as the largest conglomeration of cast-iron buildings in the world, they housed great stores and their warehouses in the nineteenth century. Other tours focus on the current vitality of the neighborhood. Most tours visit the loft residence of at least one successful artist; such residents, however, usually charge a fee for opening their houses to public scrutiny. Artists with a penchant for minimalist decor and dull colors sometimes puzzle visitors from out of town, but these unique living/working spaces always have a strong impact on people accustomed to living in conventional houses or apartments. Most of the rope-propelled or hand-operated elevators in the old factory buildings have been replaced by automatics, but the sheer cliff-style staircases that rise in the buildings are unalterable and hint at the exceptionally high ceilings in the lofts; the scale of the design for living always stuns first-time visitors. Some tours concentrate solely on the galleries, including talks with gallery owners, directors, artists, and art historians.

Before or after any organized tour of Soho or Tribeca, you should walk into a gallery and ask for the latest *Gallery Guide,* which publishes up-to-date vignettes about all the exhibits in all the galleries in town and neighboring art communities, complete with street maps and pinpointed galleries. You can explore some of these galleries on your own, guided by the pamphlet, which is usually distributed free of charge. If you have only a few hours, explore the West Broadway galleries in Soho.

Tours of Soho (some include at least a glimpse of Tribeca)

Adventure on a Shoestring, led by Howard Goldberg, visits Soho, one of Goldberg's most popular tours. Essentially, he organizes groups, which visit neighborhoods, institutions, theaters, and myriad cultural events, and he often employs on-site experts to explain the history and operations of the place in question. In Soho, therefore, you might expect him to engage gallery owners and art-world workers to talk about their universe.

Art Tours of Manhattan, as its name implies, thrives on its tours of Soho and Tribeca. The cast-iron architecture, boutiques, and restaurants take a back seat to art, which is the focus of these tours and the raison d'être for the current vitality of the neighborhood. Some of the greatest dealers in the world have their galleries here—Castelli, Sonnabend, O.K. Harris, Mary Boone, to name just a few clustered in a small section on West Broadway.

Art Tours of Manhattan, led by Barbara Guggenheim, offers a variety of tours in these and other galleries in Soho and Tribeca and also in an area northeast of Soho that the firm calls "The New Soho"; others call it "Noho," for *N*orth of *H*ouston Street.

In Tribeca, Art Tours of Manhattan visits the Clocktower, an art gallery and an occasional film and poetry-reading forum, and Franklin Furnace, a performance center, an art gallery, and an archive.

In Soho, A.T.M. comments on the nineteenth century cast-iron architecture and focuses on the art galleries with lectures about the development of the neighborhood as an art center. Groups visit prominent West Broadway galleries, with lunch or brunch in a Soho restaurant and a visit to an artist's loft or a private reception in a gallery.

In the "New Soho/Lafayette Street" area, the A.T.M. tour first visits the New York Academy of Art, then an artist's loft, and the Petersburg Press, where prints are made of works by artists such as Chia and Rauschenberg.

The A.T.M. also takes groups to galleries that serve very specifically as classrooms for beginning collectors. Three successful gallery owners in Soho talk about their skills and experiences as dealers, using works they represent to illustrate their lectures, and advise collectors on promising investment opportunities in art. Wine is served at each gallery.

A.T.M. has other custom-tailored tours for groups, which are included in the section on the Upper East Side, below.

Val Ginter conducts a tour of Soho, demonstrating his orientation as an architecture buff and an urban historian. He emphasizes the area's socioeconomic and cultural development, trying to explain that in New York City, people are generally more engrossed in the fashion and condition of their clothes, life-styles, and careers than in the exterior perfection of their buildings. Soot is not viewed as the calamity it would be on a carefully tended suburban house. And if garbage lies in piles in the heart of a Manhattan neighborhood supposed to be the quintessence of glamor, New Yorkers are rarely inspired to curtail their other activities to clean up. Mr. Ginter explains: Garbage trucks are supposed to clean up, but they do an incomplete job, which is continued by street-sweeping machines. These are even more ineffectual, since they primarily wet and scatter debris, displacing it from the center of the street into the gutters. The machines are followed by building superintendents, who may or may not live in or around the buildings they're supposed to tend. If they do, they may oversee garbage deposits put out in plastic bags for trucks and sweepers to mishandle. Ginter mentions the cleanup eccentricities of New York City in many neighborhoods, including Soho, as a subtext of Manhattan architecture and social history. (*Note:* Ginter and Barry Lewis lead similar tours in the cast-iron district, since both men essentially began their walking-tour careers for the Friends of Cast Iron Architecture, a group spearheaded by Margot Gayle; her book on cast-iron architecture influenced these two leaders directly.)

Michael Levin's tour of Soho is the most offbeat of all. He stresses the facade of the neighborhood. Saying that he presents "A Subtext of Soho: Merchandising," Levin describes the neighborhood as an example of life as an imitation of art. (The classical, Aristotelian view is that art is an imitation of life.) "But in Soho," Levin explains, "it's all about art, no matter what it is that people are selling—shoes, haircuts, sweaters, or boots." Levin points out, for example, that stores typically display only a handful of sweaters, draping them as if they were pieces of priceless sculpture in a huge area, and price polyester jackets at several hundred dollars.

"So people who have heard about the great elegance of Soho," he remarks, "are sometimes disappointed to find rusty buildings fronted by loading docks and graffiti done by vandals on building walls on side streets." Levin tells visitors that they're encountering the difference between "elegant" and "expensive." Soho, as perceived by New Yorkers, is glamorous. "Glamor without elegance is a New York concept," he explains. Something that is frayed around the edges, such as Soho buildings or parts of Greenwich Village, can cost a great deal and appear glamorous to New Yorkers, while out-of-towners view the landscape as spartan and in need of repair and embellishment. Levin hopes that his explanation illuminates the attitude of New Yorkers for out-of-towners.

Barry Lewis, in his tours of Soho and Tribeca, dwells very little on the galleries and instead recalls the vitality of Broadway in the 1850s and 1860s as the center of Manhattan, with its cast-iron architecture. In that era, the city's great department stores were housed here. Later in the century, Soho became the city's wholesaling district. Architects no longer designed their cast-iron buildings to look like little palaces; instead, they became more functional looking—"mechanistic," as Mr. Lewis says, typifying the style as "Victorian Modern." He recounts the entire history of cast-iron architecture, noting that people finally became proud of it and stopped feeling that they had to disguise it as marble.

Arthur Marks in Soho focuses on architecture, fashion, art, food, and design—his favorite topics—as he takes groups along West Broadway, the main street of Soho and Tribeca, and arranges for people to visit private loft residences.

The Municipal Art Society sometimes schedules tours of Soho as part of an eclectic walking-tour menu often geared to M.A.S. neighborhood-preservation goals. Emphases vary from season to season.

The Museum of the City of New York conducts a tour that begins at the corner of Canal Street and Broadway in Soho, passes some of the cast-iron buildings—warehouses, old cafés, and former great hotels and stores, and continues over the Brooklyn Bridge to Fulton Landing, where Walt Whitman worked for the *Brooklyn Eagle* newspaper as a journalist. The tour, called "Soho to Brooklyn," stresses the history of the Civil War era, in which Whitman takes center stage as a partisan political activist and a brilliant poet. The tour attempts to see the city through the eyes of Whitman and includes readings from his poetry about the city. Hope Cooke, former queen of Sikkim and now in charge of the museum's walking tours' program, feels that Whitman was the definitive "city poet" and a tour guide par excellence through his poetry.

New York Walkabout calls Soho "New York's Left Bank," pointing out its current role as a center for bringing artists and galleries together, cafés, restaurants, galleries, and boutiques. The firm presents the same tour several times during walking-tour season. Tours take place twice a day, once in the morning at 11:00 A.M. and again at 2:00 P.M. in the afternoon.

The 92nd Street "Y" offers a lecture and walking tour of Soho as part of an educational series given by Barry Lewis, an architectural historian who has trained many New York City guides. The "Y" offers other tours of Soho and Tribeca, too. Call for the schedule, which changes each year but always includes at least one tour of these areas.

Viewpoint International, in its roster of high-priced tours for small groups, takes you to Soho and Tribeca by bus and escorts you to the galleries, where you meet with both the wheelers and dealers and the artists in the dynamic art world. This is a typical convention-package service.

Upper East Side

The Upper East Side reigns, in the style of Elizabeth II, as a queen among queenly neighborhoods. Pockets of urban blight are few and far between and exist primarily east of Lexington Avenue. From Fifth Avenue across Madison and Park avenues to Lexington, the Upper East Side consists of stately mansions and charming townhouses. Surprises abound; on East 92nd Street, between Park and Lexington, you'll find two wooden houses—rarities in New York. They appear especially striking, once you have spent hours absorbed in observing and visiting limestone palazzo after brownstone after brick mansion.

Some tours concentrate on the mansions and churches of Fifth Avenue. Guides explain how the gentry pushed uptown during the mid-

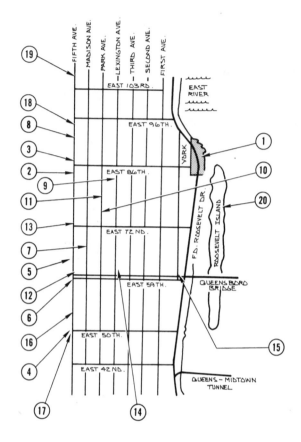

Points of Interest in the Upper East Side

1. Gracie Mansion and Carl Shurz Park
2. Metropolitan Museum of Art
3. Guggenheim Museum
4. Radio City Music Hall
5. Central Park Zoo
6. Grand Army Plaza
7. Temple Emanuel
8. Church of the Heavenly Rest
9. Headquarters of Art Tours of Manhattan
10. Whitney Museum of American Art
11. Carlyle Hotel
12. Plaza Hotel
13. Frick Collection
14. Bloomingdale's
15. Sutton Place area
16. Fifth Avenue
17. St. Patrick's Cathedral
18. Fifth Avenue mansions
19. Museum of the City of New York
20. Roosevelt Island

nineteenth to the early twentieth centuries and built magnificent houses for single, very wealthy, socially prominent families. The less affluent and less socially prominent, including members of minority groups, immigrants, and entertainers, found their niche on the Upper West Side.

Tours usually visit one small section of the Upper East Side at a time; the East Sixties, East Seventies, East Eighties, and East Nineties constitute separate tours. A tour guide can focus on any of these sections and illuminate the general ambience of the entire quarter. Some guides stress the architectural styles and life-styles of the area's first residents. Other guides focus on the current residents and what they pay to live there. For example, Arthur Marks, who has designed all the tours for the New-York Historical Society, tells you that publishing magnate Rupert Murdoch owns a multimillion dollar triplex on Fifth Avenue near the Guggenheim Museum. The maintenance cost of a $1 million apartment in this neighborhood is about $2,000 a month. And brownstone buildings cost a minimum of $1.5 million—possibly a low estimate in the late 1980s.

Art Tours of Manhattan has its headquarters here in an elegant townhouse at 63 E. 82nd Street. Some tours start here, a convenient location for visiting uptown galleries and many of the city's major art museums. In the townhouse, you walk up one gray-carpeted flight to the second floor, where you will find a reception room painted in muted colors. For private parties and tours, the firm sets up a catered buffet table of snacks, which can constitute a light dinner: caviar canapés, fashionable salads with endive or arugula, green pasta with pesto sauce, cheeses, fried chicken and vegetables for dipping, stuffed grape leaves, cheese sticks with a mildly spicy tomato sauce, wine, and mineral water. Smoking is not permitted.

Barbara Guggenheim delivers some of the lectures before scheduled tours. Sometimes guest lecturers with excellent credentials, who work at prestigious museums, substitute for her. For example, Lynn Shapiro, an art historian on the staff of the Whitney Museum of American Art, has narrated a slide show on a group tour of a museum exhibition. These talks are excellent conduits to the richness of the art tours.

"Wild Man" Steve Brill conducts edible-weed-spotting walks in Central Park, where he was once arrested for leading private tours and charging people independently of the park's authority. When the furor died down, Brill, an adept amateur botanist, was hired by the New York Department of Parks and Recreation to conduct his tours free of charge to the public. Occasionally, Mr. Brill begins his Central Park tours from a Fifth Avenue entrance to the park in the Seventies. More often he starts at 72nd Street and Central Park West. See page 141 for a detailed description of his outings.

Classical America tours, now led by Michael George for the group founded by Henry Hope Reed, focus on the area's fine classical architecture, with lectures based upon Reed's notes and books. George is capable of delivering a whole tour on one block, claims. Analyzing the architectural style of the buildings and recounting the history of the development of the block, George varies his selection of routes in a single neighborhood from year to year. If he chooses the upper reaches of the Upper East Side, he might point out the contrast between the classical building that houses the Metropolitan Museum of Art at 82nd Street and Fifth Avenue and the modern Solomon R. Guggenheim Museum building—a completely circular shape—on Fifth Avenue between 88th and 89th streets, as Reed has chosen to do in his book, *The Golden City* (W.W. Norton Co.). Lower down on the East Side, George might refer to the book's comparison of some buildings intended as private residences—one "a handsome home designed in the classical style," in 1924, for David Rockefeller at 146 E. 65th Street, the other a 1949 Philip Johnson building at 242 E. 52nd Street, which Reed describes in the following unenthusiastic way: "The front consists of a first-story wall of glazed orange brown brick surmounted by three picture windows having curtains that are always drawn."

George notes that many Europeans have come here to study American interpretations of classical forms, while Americans rarely understand them or pay enough attention to the American accomplishments.

Val Ginter, who heads his own firm, Ginter-Gotham Urban History, conducts a 57th Street tour from river to river, passing by Hell's Kitchen's northern border, arriving at the luxury of Fifth Avenue and the great stores, including Tiffany's, and going on to the northern border of the elite residential area, Sutton Place, on the Far East Side, among the most prestigious of Manhattan's neighborhoods. Ginter also leads custom-tailored tours of the entire Upper East Side for groups on request.

Barry Lewis leads a "Fifth Avenue Mile" tour, which includes excellent examples of every kind of Beaux Arts architecture. He also talks about the families who built the grand houses and how they got the money to do so. He then takes his groups off the avenue and behind the Metropolitan Museum into Central Park, where he explains the design and function of the park and its importance to the city. In Lewis's view, the park is an original American attempt to try to tame the city.

Arthur Marks gives tours of the "East Fifties, Fashionable Fifth Avenue," of the "East Sixties, Mansions and Clubhouses," and of the "East Seventies, the Fashionable East Side." His East Fifties tour begins at St. Patrick's Cathedral, with excursions into side streets, and ends at the Plaza Hotel at 59th Street and Fifth Avenue, still considered one of the world's greatest hotels. The East Sixties tour starts at Hunter College on Park Avenue between 68th and 69th streets and continues to the Seventh Regiment Armory on Park Avenue, to Temple Emanu-El on Fifth Avenue facing Central Park, to the Church of St. Vincent Ferrer, and the townhouse of the Franklin D. Roosevelts, then ends at the Metropolitan Club at 1 E. 60th Street.

The Museum of the City of New York, which is located on the northern fringe of the Gold Coast, gives walking tours of its own neighborhood. The Museum calls its Upper East Side tour "Urban Chateaux: Fifth Avenue" and begins on the steps of St. Patrick's Cathedral, at Fifth Avenue between 51st and 52nd streets.

Tourists may find it hard to believe that the development of this church, which is now in the midst of ceaseless traffic, was slow alongside the great man-made park, Central Park, designed by Olmsted and

Vaux. The newly rich tycoons of the era blazed a trail here, with exceptional energy and pioneer spirits. The multiplicity of historic architectural styles dazzles viewers on this avenue; and the grandeur was made possible in part because the income tax laws were not enacted until after the houses were built.

The New-York Historical Society tour begins officially at Frank Lloyd Wright's Guggenheim Museum, a circular building that Wright reportedly built to prove the superiority of architecture over painting, drawing, and sculpture. The exhibits are indeed often overshadowed by the spectacular museum itself, which faces Fifth Avenue between 88th and 89th streets.

From the Guggenheim, the group looks northward to the National Academy of Design, which was built as a palace in 1901 to house the family of Archer Milton Huntington of the Southern Pacific Railroad fortune. Ordinarily, people pass these buildings with the thought: oh, those are public buildings. But the tour reminds you that single families (Carnegies, Posts, Kahns, etc.) once lived in privacy and opulence here, rather the way Victor Hugo lived on the Place de Vosges in Paris. And the graceful sweep of the marble staircase arching up from the formal entranceway in the Huntington mansion makes you pensive about the life-styles of the elegant couples who climbed to balls and parties; a majordomo announced them by name at the entrance.

The Academy stands next to the Episcopal Church of the Heavenly Rest, designed in Gothic Art Deco style in 1927–29 by the same architects who consulted in the Moorish Art Deco design of Temple Emanu-El nearly thirty blocks downtown on Fifth Avenue. The church has no steeple because (according to Arthur Marks) Mrs. Andrew Carnegie, who lived just to the north, "didn't want the shadow of a steeple crossing her tennis court."

This neighborhood's private grandeur had to go public after the 1929 Depression. Although the income tax was instituted in 1913, it wasn't really effective until the financial structure of the country changed in the 1930s. At that point, the life-styles of the wealthy altered radically to protect their fortunes.

Upper East Side

New York Walkabout sponsors an all-in-one tour of Sutton and Beekman places and Turtle Bay, three prestigious neighborhoods on the Upper East Side of Manhattan, running from the East Forties to 59th Street. Quite a few celebrities have lived here: Huntington Hartford on Beekman Place, Irving Berlin on Sutton Place—Greta Garbo—Katharine Hepburn. Offered several times a year, in spring, summer, and fall, the tours begin at 11:00 A.M. and 2:00 P.M.

The **92nd Street "Y"** conducts a variety of tours on the Upper East Side. One focuses on several painters who have studios in the neighborhood and open them to tour groups there. Max Ferguson, one of the artists, conducts the tour for the "Y" himself. Several art tours take place in the Whitney Museum of American Art on Madison Avenue at 75th Street, under the auspices of the "Y," separate from the Whitney's own tours.

The "Y" also sponsors such tours as "Gracie Mansion and Yorkville." Yorkville's main street is E. 86th street, from Fifth Avenue to York Avenue. The tour highlights the area's German and Middle European ambience, with German and Czech restaurants among the ethnic attractions, and the great mansions where the Astors and the Rhinelanders once spent their summers and beer breweries once thrived. (Now Manhattan's only brewery is in Soho.) Another tour visits the official residence of the mayor, Gracie Mansion, which was chosen for Fiorello LaGuardia.

"Millionaire's Mile: Fifth Avenue Mansions" is a "Y" tour, which views, from their exteriors, mansions designed by renowned architects for famous families—the Whitneys, Vanderbilts, and their contemporaries—in an era when servants had more space to live in than today's Yuppies and Dinks (Dual-Income-No-Kids).

The **New York Park Rangers** lead a variety of tours in Central Park on weekends, often beginning at Belvedere Castle (opposite 77th Street in the middle of the park) but quite often starting at other sites, such as the Dairy (near E. 66th Street and Fifth Avenue). The focus of these tours varies from weather prediction to flora and fauna, bird-watching, photography techniques, park development and design, and many other specialties of the knowledgeable Rangers.

Sutton Area Community, Inc. sponsors several tours a year of this prestigious little enclave, one of the wealthiest neighborhoods in town. (Sutton Place runs from the Queensboro Bridge at 59th Street down to 53rd Street, along Sutton Place, east of First Avenue.) From wide alleyways between some of the buildings, you can get a close-up view of the East River. Tour leaders usually know anecdotes about the architectural, social, and political history of the neighborhood; current issues that will bring about any changes in the life-styles of the residents usually engage their attention as well. And in wafting perfumes and Burberry trenchcoats, "locals" take the tours themselves. The S.A.C. has sponsored shows of historic photographs of the Sutton Place area and lectures on the neighborhood as part of the group's goal of reveling in the luxury and preserving the elite image of the enclave. Val Ginter has been among the professional tour leaders hired by the neighborhood group to give talks or lead walks.

John Tauranac, a writer, guide, and consultant to the Metropolitan Transportation Authority, teaches at New York University's School of Continuing Education; his love affair with New York City centers upon its architecture. On the "Gold Coast," Mr. Tauranac, actually a city generalist, leads a walk roaming from the Carnegie Mansion on 91st Street and Fifth Avenue down to the Rhinelander House at 72nd Street and Madison Avenue. The walk, which is one mile long, takes three hours. The history of the Rhinelander House, which emerges in the detailed lecture, is the type of tale that makes the neighborhood come alive. The house was built by Gertrude Rhinelander Waldo, who saw many chateaus in Europe in 1899, while she was on her honeymoon. She ordered a house built for herself along the lines of these magnificent structures. Her husband died before the family could move in, however, and neither Mrs. Waldo nor her son, who became a New York City Police Commissioner, ever lived there. When she died, a bank took over the house and tried to rent it, but it was not inhabited until 1922. Since then it has housed several fashionable clients, from art and antique dealers to the current tenant, Polo/Ralph Lauren.

Wall Street

As it was in the beginning, so it is in the end, or at least up to now. The self-containment of historic Wall Street and the surrounding area hasn't changed entirely since it was a Dutch Colony in the seventeenth century. Unlike explorers who sought religious freedom or riches for a kingdom, the Dutch West India Company sent diverse European nationals to the tip of Manhattan Island solely to do business—and that remains Wall Street's raison d'être today. At dawn, business workers begin the rush to their offices. The rest of the city wakes up and goes to bed later, almost as if it existed in a different time zone. On weekends, restaurants and stores in the Wall Street area close. Only the renovated historic South Street Seaport, about a fifteen-minute walk north of Wall Street, attracts tourists to its lively restaurants, boutiques, and an exhibit of old sailing ships, including the Ambrose Lightship, which used to light the harbor at night. In warm weather, tourists sun themselves at outdoor cafés and on ferryboats during the day and stretch out at night for concerts on the old piers.

Organized tours amble around this historic nucleus of Manhattan. Often they start on Wall Street, once the site of an actual wall erected by the Dutch, which stretched from the East to the Hudson rivers. The other site of major interest in this area is City Hall, a pretty French Renaissance and Federal-style palace, built in 1811, one of the city's finest public buildings.

Walk up the wide front steps; right away you'll notice two elegant, curved marble stairways dominating the foyer, complementing each other under a dome. They lead to formal rooms and museums where portraits of notables from Colonial days and the days of the young Republic hang, above the first-floor offices. When you are outside again, note that the Statue of Justice on the dome has no blindfold. Local wits insist that she must keep her eyes open because of the corrupt characters who come and go here.

City Hall faces a triangular park called City Hall Park, originally known as the Common. An old statue of Nathan Hale says he was executed in the Common, though historians disagree. Patriots held a

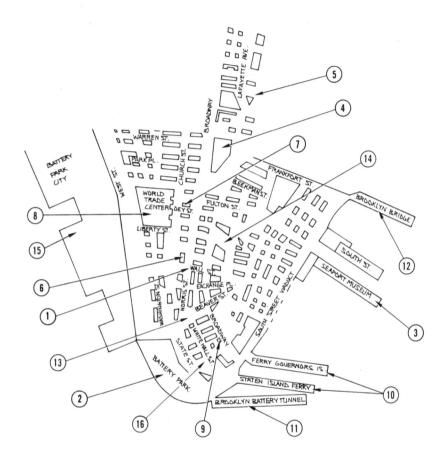

Points of Interest in Historic New York

1. Wall Street
2. Battery Park
3. South Street Seaport
4. City Hall
5. Civic Center
6. Trinity Church
7. St. Paul's Chapel
8. World Trade Center
9. Fraunces Tavern

10. Ferries to Governor's Island and Staten Island
11. Brooklyn Battery Tunnel
12. Brooklyn Bridge
13. Bowling Green
14. Federal Reserve Bank
15. Battery Park City
16. Peter Minuit Plaza

rally in the Common and decided to send delegates to the Continental Congress in 1774. Two years later, George Washington's troops assembled here to hear a reading of the Declaration of Independence. A few weeks later they were forced out of town and could not return until the end of the Revolutionary War.

If you face City Hall, to your right you will see the huge, U-shaped Municipal Building, erected in 1913 to house the many individuals hired to deal with paperwork generated by the incorporation of Brooklyn, Queens, Staten Island, and the Bronx into New York City. Beyond the Municipal Building stand the Foley Square courthouses, which make up a somberly majestic Civic Center. Some tours focus on this area.

For earlier, historic sights, tours concentrate on more southerly points, beginning with the 1766 St. Paul's Chapel, one of the oldest public buildings in the city at the corner of Fulton Street, about ten minutes from City Hall. George Washington attended services here, after being sworn in as president in 1789. His pew is marked. Royalty and world leaders have prayed here, too. A pristine graveyard flanks the church. And on Mondays and Thursdays, the public can listen to free noontime concerts in the sanctuary.

Further down Broadway, at Rector Street, Trinity Church, facing Wall Street's western end, also presents lunchtime concerts. Many Wall Streeters come here to relax and escape the pressures of their jobs. Trinity was rebuilt twice, once because of a horrendous fire, and again when the structure almost collapsed under the weight of snow. The current Gothic Revival masterpiece dates back to 1846. Alexander Hamilton was buried in the graveyard, after he was fatally wounded in a duel with Aaron Burr. At the time, dueling was so frowned upon that Hamilton was reluctant to fight, and the church nearly banned his burial. He was saved by an antidueling tract he had written not long before his death.

The side streets on the west side of Broadway allow you an awesome, close-up view of the cylinders of the World Trade Center. Windows on the World, the 107th-floor restaurant located atop 1 World Trade Center and decorated in pretty pastel colors to offset the excitement of the height, is open every day. Tour leaders point out the World Trade Center and Battery Park City and sometimes visit them for the excitement of the sky bridges connecting the World Trade Center to the World Financial Center in Battery Park City. These structures also afford tour groups the opportunity of seeing how a "new city" was built on landfill on the river.

Across the street from Trinity Church, Wall Street begins on the site of a wall that went up here in 1635 and was abandoned in 1669, because it always needed repairs. Eventually the British tore it down. One block's walk brings you to 11 Wall Street, a bright corner entrance to the New York Stock Exchange. A sign directs visitors to 20 Broad Street for a free tour during weekday business hours. You'll have a view from a gallery of the trading floor in full action. Guides such as Marvin Gelfand and James Kaplan are especially adept at explaining the history of the great economic institutions of Wall Street.

Also at the corner of Wall and Broad Streets stands a Doric-pillared temple, Federal Hall National Memorial, built in 1834–1842. It is an excellent example of Greek Revival style in New York. George Washington took his oath of office on the spot where his statue now stands. Inside, the rotunda and a museum are open, free of charge, to the public. The memorial is usually open from May through September, Sundays through Fridays, from 9:00 A.M. to 4:30 P.M., at no charge.

You can walk straight down Wall Street, looking at banks and office buildings, listening to anecdotes about the area's architectural, social, economic, and political development recounted by the guides. (On winter walks, which are few and far between, the steam rising from underground pipes gives you the romantic illusion that you're in foggy London town.) Veering right on Pearl Street, near the bottom of Wall, you'll soon come to Hanover Square and, facing it, at 56 Beaver Street, Delmonico's, a legendary restaurant on this site since 1838. To underscore its historic status, the current owners have framed Delmonico's first printed menu from 1834 (in another building) and hung it on a wall in an elegant, low-keyed dining room. You'll notice that Wall Street restaurants have a more sedate, conservative mien than the more frankly glamorous restaurants in newer parts of town. Delmonico's serves breakfast, lunch, and dinner; call 422–4747 for a reservation.

If you have already turned off Wall Street onto Broad Street and walked south, you will come to Fraunces Tavern, an old brick tavern renovated many times since its construction by the Dutch sometime around 1700. It has stood on this site—where Pearl and Broad streets converge—for centuries. All the tour guides point out the tavern; it has a house specialty—Baked Chicken Washington, with mushrooms in a light cream sauce *en casserole au gratin*—one of the menu's most economical entrées. "Oh, yes, Washington loved this recipe," a tavern host says, assuring you of its authenticity with his tongue in his cheek. "It was easy for him to chew with his wooden teeth."

In the afternoon, the bar sets out free snacks including cheeses, chips, sausages, and other goodies. On two upstairs floors, you will find a room designed to look like the Dutch tavern where the colony's businessmen met to conduct affairs and to gossip. Eventually, the tavern served as Washington's headquarters, where he said farewell to his troops in 1783. A museum on the top floor has special exhibits about Colonial days. Although the restaurant closes on weekends, the museum is open on Sundays. For reservations in the wood-paneled dining room, with its working fireplace and roomy leather armchairs, call 269–0144; for the museum's schedule, call 425–1778.

A few blocks downtown at Bowling Green, Broadway begins, near the Customs House, a political and economic force in nineteenth century New York. Certain individuals became very wealthy presiding over the Customs House by skimming money off the import taxes collected on goods entering the country. Before the institution of the federal income tax, the Customs House served as the most important source of revenue for the federal government; two-thirds of its revenue came from New York harbor. At one time, Chester A. Arthur headed the Customs House (and was fired for incompetence). Eight years later he became U.S. President. Another president, Rutherford B. Hayes, tried to have his buddy from society circles, Theodore Roosevelt, Sr., appointed head of the Customs House. Later, "trust-buster" President Theodore Roosevelt, Jr., won a twenty-year battle to force the breakup of Rockefeller's Standard Oil Co., which by 1910 had consolidated 90 percent of the world's oil.

Nearby at Bowling Green, Peter Minuit of the Dutch West India Company paid $24 to the Indians for Manhattan. The full value of taxable real estate in Manhattan reached about $272 billion in 1988.

After any tour, you can take a 25¢ ferry ride to Staten Island: it's as scenic and relaxing as it's supposed to be. Some tours include it in their schedules.

Despite the immutable historic character of the area, the tour leaders have varied approaches. In fact, you can take several tours and not repeat the same material appreciably. Most of the generalists have at least one Wall Street-area tour in their repertoires, whether they concentrate on the architecture on Broadway, or a Revolutionary War battle site, or the growth of New York's harbor.

Here's a sampling of Wall Street tours.

Classical America's Michael George leads various tours of the neighborhood. Though he concentrates on architecture, he touches on the people and the history of the neighborhood as well. Because many people who take Classical America tours are repeat visitors, Mr. George never takes exactly the same route twice. For the N.Y.U. School of Continuing Education's noncredit course and for the New-York Historical Society subgroups that he leads under the direction of Arthur Marks, Mr. George plots a straightforward tour, visiting the best-known historic sites.

In the Civic Center, he observes that the various courthouse buildings were designed by different architects, all keeping an eye on one another. So the Municipal Building and the Federal and State courthouses have Corinthian columns, even though the buildings are independent of each other. All are classical, public buildings, richly ornamented and filled with carved allegorical figures telling the history of the justice system, in a variety of building materials—marble, granite, limestone, and wood. George talks about the construction of the Municipal Building at the time of the consolidation of New York City in the early years of the twentieth century, the history of the ticker-tape parades, and the renovations of the buildings. He includes the Tweed Courthouse, named for Boss Tweed of the influential Tammany Society political group, and the Surrogate Courthouse behind the Tweed.

Libby Corydon, an adept multilingual tour guide, usually confines herself to weekend walks to accommodate her full-time job as a manager with American Express. Ms. Corydon has led tours for the travel and tourism industry, for private clients, and for major cultural institutions. A generalist, she nevertheless has some pet tours.

She particularly likes to lead groups from Lower Manhattan across the Brooklyn Bridge in the late afternoon to arrive at Brooklyn Heights's promenade as the lights in Lower Manhattan begin to glow and dominate the darkening sky. With a degree in American civilization, she can talk about the city's architecture and social development, sprinkling her lecture with insider's details such as the introduction of mansard roofs; long popular in France, the roof style kept the houses smaller in outside appearance than they actually were, so French owners could avoid taxation in the nineteenth century. In New York, the style became very fashionable.

Federal Hall National Memorial, 28 Wall Street at Nassau Street, facing Broad Street, was completed in 1842, according to the city's Landmarks Commission, in the heart of the financial district. George Washington took his oath of office on the spot where his statue stands outside. Inside is a rotunda and a museum including Washington memorabilia. Call 264–8711 to assure yourself of the schedule.

The **Federal Reserve Bank,** 33 Liberty Street, has more gold in its underground vault than Fort Knox. You can tour the bank free of charge on one of its own guided tours, if you reserve a place at least a week in advance. Tours are given from Monday through Friday, at 10:00 A.M., 11:00 A.M., 1:00 P.M., and 2:00 P.M., and begin with a talk about security. You then see money being counted and shredded, view a collection of historic coins, and, as the highlight, visit the gold vault.

Val Ginter's Ginter-Gotham Urban History conducts an unusual tour of this historic district, concentrating on its art deco architecture. Sometimes Ginter combines the Wall Street district with midtown Manhattan in a bus tour of art deco landmarks. Downtown, he points out the Downtown Athletic Club, designed by Starrett and Van Vleck; the cantilevered corners here presage the profile of the Citicorp Building in midtown. The same architects designed the Bloomingdale's building up-town. At 29 Broadway, Ginter points out the art deco verticals, horizontals, and spirals around the entrance. The Irving Trust Building at 1 Wall Street is a fine example of "bankers art deco." The former Cities Service Building, at 70 Pine Street, is topped by a crystalline lighting fixture. Ginter claims this building did for downtown what the Chrysler Building did for midtown. The former Insurance Center Building at 80 John Street was selected as one of two American art deco buildings for entry in the 1925 Berlin Exhibition. The other entry was the Barclay-Vesey Building at 140 West Street, designed for the telephone company. And there are others, either in art deco style or paving the way for this style, all erected during the decade beginning around 1925.

Marvin Gelfand's Walk of the Town Wall Street Tour appeared in the form of an article in the November 1987 issue of *American Heritage* Magazine. Gelfand, an economic historian and a professional guide with his own firm, set forth his view of "the street." On this tour, he outlines his version of the street's growth and the development of its major financial institutions, stressing the fact that politics are an integral part of the street's culture.

He likes to start his tours at 10:00 A.M. at Trinity Church, mentioning, among many points of interest, Alexander Hamilton's tomb near the southern fence; the events leading up to Hamilton's demise; and Aaron Burr's hindsight about the duel in which he killed Hamilton.

From there, Gelfand heads directly for the Irving Trust Company at 1 Wall Street, a glittering white, fifty-five-story limestone building, the last to be built directly on Wall Street, in 1932. Washington Irving lived on the site while he was writing *A History of New York, from the Beginning of the World to the End of the Dutch Dynasty.* Irving was 26 when the history was published in 1809. Irving nicknamed New York "Gotham" and coined the phrase about its love of "the almighty dollar," in the days when Wall Street was still a modest commercial and banking center, in 1808. The bank bears his name.

Gelfand illuminates the complexities of Wall Street's development, telling tales of the individual buildings and the financial wizards who shaped the destiny of the country and the world—among them, J. P.

Morgan, H. B. Hyde of Equitable Life Assurance, and, as Gelfand's describes him, "the man who stood in awe of himself," Bernard Baruch. Gelfand also tells about the agreement signed in 1792 by twenty-one individuals and representatives of three firms, who gathered under a buttonwood tree that used to stand on Wall Street. The first stockbrokers, they agreed that none of them would buy at public auction; none would trade at a rate of less than one-quarter percent commission. And they would give each other preference in their dealings. This brokers' fraternity evolved into the New York Stock Exchange.

Gelfand's expertise makes his tour one of the most educational excursions into the street.

Joyce Gold, a teacher, writer, and tour leader, with a master's degree in metropolitan studies from New York University, specializes in four areas of Manhattan. One of them is the financial district, about which she has written a book called *From Windmills to the World Trade Center: A Walking Guide to Lower Manhattan History.* It is available for $3.50 plus $1 for mailing from Ms. Gold, Old Warren Road Press, 141 W. 17th Street, New York, NY 10011. Gold's favorite period in Manhattan, she has said, ranges from the Dutch settlement in 1624 to the end of the American Revolution in 1783.

The financial district, she explains, was once the outskirts of New Amsterdam, where the streets were essentially laid out by the Dutch. The street names were derived from the early condition of the terrain: Beaver Street had beavers; Stone Street was paved; Mill Street had a windmill; Pearl Street's merchants sold pearly-shelled oysters; the Dutch put up a wall on Wall Street; Jews Alley, later called Mill Lane, which intersects with Mill St., was a Jewish ghetto, where Lehman Brothers originally built its headquarters. The first synagogue in New York was built in 1730 on Mill Street, which is now called South William. A plaque on a garage commemorates the synagogue's existence.

Gold talks about the Episcopal roots of New York, dating back to the mid-seventeenth century, and about Castle Garden (now called Castle Clinton), which served as the New York State landing station from 1855 to 1890.

She starts the tour at Trinity Church, moves to the Battery, and ends up at the South Street Seaport—a long walk in which she uses a chronological approach to give a sense of the progression of changes in the district.

James Kaplan leads a few unique tours of Lower Manhattan to mark historic anniversaries. In the Wall Street area, he documents the economic rise of New York, and at City Hall, he outlines the city's political history. Elements of both tours interweave at times, since he sees economic and political developments as inexorably bound together. A tax lawyer and economic historian, he uses his tours as jumping-off points to present his opinions.

He leads a Wall Street tour, usually given at the beginning of November, to memorialize the opening of the Erie Canal in 1825—"a seminal event for the growth of New York City," he says accurately. He starts at Bowling Green and the U.S. Customs House, the site of the first Dutch colony and its fort. From there he walks to Battery Park, then to Castle Clinton National Monument, a fort built to protect New York harbor during the War of 1812; there he gives a long discourse on the Erie Canal.

By that point he has already given the background of the sale of Manhattan Island by the Indians, (who didn't actually own it); discussed the relations between the British and the Dutch in the colony; progressed through the Revolutionary War. At Castle Clinton, he discusses the rise of the Tammany Society, stressing its early positive aspects. As it rose in influence, it became synonymous in people's minds with political graft, but Mr. Kaplan points out that at its inception, it championed the rights of the poor. DeWitt Clinton, originally a Tammany man, later a key opponent of Tammany Hall, was instrumental in the building of the Erie Canal, which linked Lake Erie with the Atlantic Ocean. The canal was a very important part of his tenure as governor of New York and his re-election campaign: It changed the economic fortunes of New York City.

The tour moves on to South Ferry, where Kaplan talks about the growth of private enterprise in town, beginning with Cornelius Vanderbilt and his empire. A courageous, skilled boatman, he made a trip to

Sandy Hook without being stopped by the British during the War of 1812. With that same sort of enterprising spirit, he became the richest man in America, controlling first the steamboats, then the trains. By the time he died, he had built a fortune of about $200 million at a time when the average annual income for Americans was about $200.

The tour continues to the U.S. Customs House, a great Beaux Arts building. (Kaplan touches lightly upon architectural styles, focusing instead on human drama.) From there, the tour goes to the corner of Wall and Broad streets, and the lecture turns to J.P. Morgan & Co., whose headquarters are at 23 Wall. (J.P. Morgan was to finance what Rockefeller was to oil.) The tour ends at the I.T.T. Building, with lecture/patter about the firm as the fourth largest conglomerate before divestiture in the 1960s.

Kaplan leads his City Hall-area tour annually on the Sunday closest to the date of the founding of the Tammany Society: May 12, 1789. The Tammany Society sprang up as a reaction to elitism. Founded by William Mooney, the Society had Aaron Burr as its first notable leader. Kaplan puts forth the view that the three most important dates in New York history were the founding of the Tammany Society, July 4, 1776, and evacuation day—the day on which the British left town, November 25, 1783. Kaplan's tour attempts to celebrate the founding of Tammany Society as synonymous with the rise of the democratic tradition in city government.

An early, primary goal—and eventual victory—of the Tammany Society was to give every man the right to vote, regardless of whether or not he owned property. (Until 1824 a man had to own property to be eligible to vote.) From City Hall Park, Kaplan walks to the U.S. Customs House and talks about its influence, central to the development of New York City, and its links to national politics and the involvement of Tammany Hall.

Kaplan usually leads his tour under the aegis of the 92nd Street "Y."

In 1988 James Kaplan inaugurated his newest tour, about the rise of Wall Street and its great crashes. It is actually the story of the rise of capital in the United States, beginning with the Dutch West India Company, the first real capitalistic company in the modern world. Kaplan tracks the rise of J. P. Morgan in the nineteenth century, President Theodore Roosevelt's trust-busting, and the recent rise of junk bonds, pioneered by Drexel Burnham. He also discusses the founding and development of various banks. He begins the tour, which will take place in October once a year—commemorating the month in which the two most notable crashes occurred—at the U.S. Customs House.

Jeffrey Kroessler, a Queens specialist, leads one Manhattan tour—"City Hall/Tammany Hall Walk"—which begins at City Hall Park, goes to the Tweed Courthouse, the Municipal Building, and then heads north to the once very seamy Five Points district at the southern tip of Chinatown. The walk continues into Chinatown for a look at the nineteenth-century tenements that, for the most part, still house new (Chinese) immigrants currently flooding in in large numbers. Kroessler talks about the predecessors of the Chinese on this tour; in the nineteenth century, the majority of immigrants came from Italy, Ireland, Germany, and Eastern Europe. The walk ends at the Al Smith House on Oliver Street, where Smith, a former governor of New York, was raised.

Michael Levin's Wall Street tour focuses on the year 1790. In that year, New York City was the capital of the United States. In Levin's view, the eighteenth century was therefore a high point for New York culture. Levin tries to restrict his walk to the territory that he knows George Washington covered on foot. He calls his tour "In Washington's Footsteps." Within these parameters, Levin focuses on Trinity Church, Federal Hall National Memorial, and some of the narrowest streets in the district: William, South William, and Stone streets. Stone Street, only twelve feet wide, makes Levin aware of what it felt like to live in New York City in Colonial days. He also takes people to the only archaeological site in downtown Manhattan—the excavated foundation of the Dutch City Hall, which was called the *Stadt Huys*.

Barry Lewis tailors his tours to the requests of various groups, because the financial district is so vast; he can't encompass the whole area in a single tour. One tour in his repertoire is called "From Bowling Green to

City Hall"—a walk beginning at the Battery's Castle Clinton and the nearby neighborhood, which was once an extremely fashionable residential spot. He continues along Park Row, once dubbed "Newspaper Row," to Greek Revival Wall Street, Neo-Gothic Trinity Church, and the World Trade Center, ending the walk at City Hall.

This itinerary is just a bare sketch of the tour given by Mr. Lewis, a mesmerizing guide and architectural historian who is well versed in the social, political, and economic history of all the neighborhoods he tours.

Richard McDermott, publisher of the *New York Chronicle,* a quarterly by and for New York City tour guides, leads a Water Street and South Street Seaport tour. Along Water Street, he points out Belgian block streets—granite blocks quarried primarily in New England and hand-prepared to resemble the blocks with which the Belgians paved their streets beginning in the early nineteenth century. McDermott also talks about the eighteenth-century houses that have survived since the district functioned as a mercantile center. The Bridge Café, a very well kept restaurant beside the Brooklyn Bridge, built in that era, still stands, one of the oldest wooden buildings in the city.

During the Civil War, it was called the Hole in the Wall. According to legend, it had a six-foot-tall female bouncer, who carried a blackjack and a pistol. She knocked men unconscious, bit their ears off, and put them in a pickling bottle behind the bar. The rustic-looking successor, the Bridge Café, still keeps a jar with a plastic ear behind the bar for old-times' sake.

In the neighborhood, too, a gang leader named Kit Burns had a rat pack in the 1860s, with his headquarters two doors south of the Hole in the Wall; the headquarters still stands—an old brick-fronted building in need of repair. Many gangs made Water Street their headquarters in the era. When the shipping industry left, all traces of the gangs disappeared. The area was abandoned and lay in ghastly disrepair until the South Street Seaport was developed in recent years.

Joyce Mendelsohn's Fourth of July tour sets out as an overnight walk, with police escort, on the eve of the Fourth of July. On the theory that

Wall Street

the first battle of the American Revolution took place at Golden Hill, on John Street between William and Pearl streets, in January 1770, two months before the Boston Massacre, Joyce Mendelsohn visits the battle site on her tour of Lower Manhattan.

The walk begins at City Hall at 2:00 A.M. and ends at the Vietnam Veterans Memorial in Coenties Slip, near the South Street Seaport, at about 6:00 A.M. Mendelsohn extends the walk to include a Staten Island ferry ride. She led the tour herself in 1985 and 1986, though not in 1987 when, as a schoolteacher on sabbatical, she went back to school to take history courses about New York City. However, she will probably be leading the tour, which she invented, from now on. It is sponsored by the 92nd Street "Y." Sometimes fife and drum players, as well as other musicians, join the tour, and a troupe of actors re-enacts the Golden Hill battle.

The **Municipal Art Society** tour schedule includes a visit to the historic district, focusing on its development and redevelopment through the centuries; the tour leader points out the traces of the beach, forest, and early Dutch village still visible.

Another M.A.S. tour in the general vicinity goes to the Old Police Headquarters on Centre Street, a fine Beaux Arts landmark building recently converted to cooperative apartments.

The **Museum of the City of New York**'s tour traces the history of the district back to its days of dependence on the port at Manhattan's southern tip. The tour, which also visits Wall Street, is called "From Sailing Ships to Skyscrapers."

The New-York Historical Society sponsors "The World of the Constitution," a tour that begins at City Hall and proceeds through City Hall Park to St. Paul's Chapel, where the founding fathers, including Washington, Adams, Hamilton, and Hancock, worshipped. Then the group goes further downtown, along Broadway, to Trinity Church graveyard, where Alexander Hamilton is buried (far from the site where he died in a duel with Aaron Burr). The tour also visits the sites of the homes of presidents Washington, Jefferson, and Madison; Castle Clinton; and ends

84

with a reception at Federal Hall National Memorial. On that site, Washington was inaugurated as president in 1789.

The **New York Stock Exchange** has tours from Monday through Friday, beginning at 9:30 A.M., on the third floor. There's a video presentation of the workings of the New York Stock Exchange and a gallery view of the vast trading floor. For the sentimental, there's a charming gift shop, with all types of items stamped with logos of the Stock Exchange.

New York Walkabout has several tours of Lower Manhattan. The newest tour, called "A Story of Immigration," traces the history of the Jews in New York from the seventeenth-century to the late nineteenth-century, when there was an enormous wave of immigration from Eastern Europe. Sites include the city's first synagogue and Castle Clinton, which was once an immigration center at the tip of Manhattan. Other Walkabout tours of the area include "Where It All Began," a walk from Trinity Church on Broadway down to Castle Clinton, along the streets that were laid out in the city's early days; "The Past Preserved," which visits Fulton Street and the South Street Seaport's historic streets, buildings, monuments, and dockside historic sailing ships; and "Beyond the City Gates," (a reference to the area north of Wall Street, once the northern border of town), which visits City Hall, Broadway, Newspaper Row, the Woolworth Building, and St. Paul's Chapel. This last tour takes place only on prescheduled Sundays at 2:00 P.M. The other tours leave twice a day, at 11:00 A.M. and 2:00 P.M., on the Sundays that they are offered. New York Walkabout has walking tour seasons and schedules some tours several times during each season.

Joseph L. Schiff's Jewish Urban Studies Tour visits Wall Street. On the premise that a good education in the history, culture, and religion of the Jewish people exists in the streets of New York City, Schiff has developed tours of nearly a dozen neighborhoods. His Wall Street tour, which he calls "Early Jewish New York," visits the traces of the Jewish settlement in New Amsterdam. In 1654 twenty-three Jews arrived on the St. Charles boat from Recife, Brazil. For traces of that migration,

Wall Street

Schiff takes tours to the Spanish-Portuguese cemetery (dating back to 1683) in Chatham Square, now in Chinatown, north of the historic district. The cemetery belongs to the Congregation She'arith Israel, which is located at 70th Street and Central Park West. The oldest synagogue in North America, it originally stood on South William Street. Schiff leads group tours with advance reservations only.

John Tauranac, a consultant and mapmaker for the Metropolitan Transportation Authority, is also a writer and teacher at New York University and a walking-tour leader to many city neighborhoods. One of his favorite tours goes from City Hall down Broadway to the Battery. As an architectural historian, he particularly appreciates the opportunity along that route to point out good examples of just about every style of architecture in New York City, with the exception of brownstone row houses and Beaux Arts townhouses.

At Wall Street, he takes his groups to the left to see Federal Hall National Memorial, the New York Stock Exchange, and the Citibank Building, which used to be the Merchants Exchange; Isaiah Rogers was the architect, and the famous firm of McKim, Mead and White added onto the building. (Stanford White, the colorful architect who was shot by a jealous husband in Madison Square Garden in 1906, was the White in the firm.)

Chapter Five

Lower East Side
and the East Village

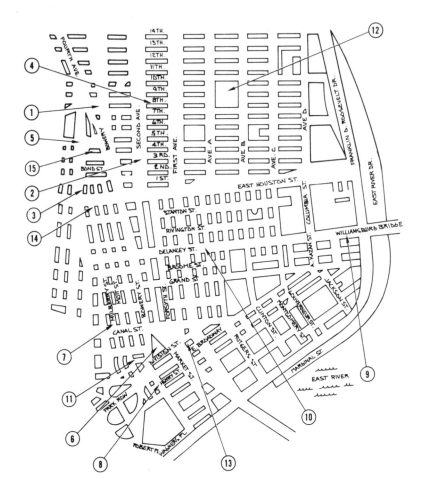

Points of Interest in the Lower East Side and East Village

1. Cooper Union
2. Second Avenue
3. Puck Building
4. St. Mark's Place/St. Mark's Church in the Bowery
5. Lafayette Street
6. Confucius Plaza and Chatham Square
7. Mulberry Street
8. Henry Street
9. Williamsburg Bridge
10. Delancey Street
11. Pell-Mott Street neighborhood
12. Tompkins Square Park
13. Eldridge Street Synagogue
14. Old St. Patrick's Cathedral
15. Old Merchant's House

Millions of people have a sentimental attachment to the Lower East Side (and the East Village contained in that neighborhood). Either their ancestors passed through or lived there for a while, or else some of the country's old-time entertainers, born and raised on the Lower East Side, shared with them their childhood memories of hard times and hilarity. Politicians whose careers had nationwide reverberations were born there. And all the ethnic groups that passed through the sprawling neighborhood have left their marks. The groups most evident today are Jews, Italians, Chinese, Ukrainians, Poles, and Hispanics, along with small numbers of West Indians, American blacks, Asian Indians, Thais, and Japanese. German and Irish immigrants passed through the neighborhood on their way uptown—the Irish to many areas, notably the Bronx and Queens, the Germans to Manhattan's Yorkville, centered on East 86th Street. And traces of their communities on the Lower East Side remain to tantalize the sharp-eyed with nostalgic feelings.

The area sprawls roughly from Broadway on the west, to the East River, and from little Columbus Park at the southern tip of Chinatown to East 14th Street. Within it, Chinatown is a little boomtown.

The neighborhoods within the Lower East Side are differentiated in the following way today: the Seward Park area (a dwindling Jewish community); Chinatown; Little Italy; Cooper Square; St. Mark's Place and the East Village, running from Second Avenue to Avenue D, containing Avenues A, B, C, and D, nicknamed Alphabet City; and the ethnic pockets of the East Village. Little Italy was once "Little Ireland," more commonly called Five Points. The Germans settled for a time on Second Avenue; their most obvious legacy was the famed 14th Street restaurant, Luchow's, which served authentic German cuisine, against a background of oompah music by strolling musicians, from the mid-1800s until 1982. The building itself dates back to the 1840s.

Almost all the major institutions have various tours to parts of the Lower East Side. Some free-lance guides have pet tours to parts of the neighborhood. And several Chinese guides conduct excellent walking tours of contemporary Chinatown.

The Chinese have kindly plunked down a big, lively Chinatown conveniently in the midst of New York City, but millions of people who visit annually know little about it except for the availability of good, low-cost sumptuous dinners and dim sum brunches.

Until 1965, when Congress made immigration quotas for the Chinese comparable to those for Europeans, the Chinese community numbered only about 20,000 in New York City and lived in virtual isolation. However, with immigration laws eased, and the lease on Hong Kong running out by 1997, ethnic Chinese from all over Southeast Asia, from Hong Kong, and even from mainland China filtering through Hong Kong, have been arriving in droves for refuge and economic stability. Now about 100,000 people live in Chinatown. Thousands more arrive daily (there are currently an estimated 350,000 Chinese living in greater New York), to work in a freewheeling atmosphere reminiscent of old-fashioned Hong Kong markets. The Chinese guides generally tell about the forces that established the enclave and make it tick today, while the generalist guides put the history of the Lower East Side's development into perspective.

Adventure on a Shoestring sponsors a casual walk through Chinatown and a dim sum lunch a few times a year. The dim sum meal allows visitors to take part in a venerable Chinese custom of sampling varied dumplings with tea at communal tables in a busy restaurant at midday on Sundays. (The Cantonese, who are such good cooks that the proverb

"Eat in Canton" is popular throughout China, invented dim sum long ago to accompany business discussions, and the custom spread throughout China, with mild Cantonese recipes as the mainstay everywhere. Dim sum is so popular and prevalent a custom that, in Hong Kong, there's even a dim sum teahouse where exotic bird dealers meet to wheel and deal.) Leader Howard Goldberg knows some charming details: for example, Irving Berlin once worked as a singing waiter on Doyers Street.

Art Tours of Manhattan may still occasionally visit, on special request of groups, the few galleries remaining in the East Village art district at the northernmost end of the Lower East Side. In the early to mid-1980s the district ran approximately from E. 2nd to E. 13th streets and from Second Avenue to Avenue C. One highly regarded gallery owner, Pat Hearn, opened a tiny showcase between avenues C and D in the mid-1980s—the easternmost gallery of the enclave. Most East Village galleries ranged in size from tiny to small. And some of the most whimsical artifacts in them were the desks, lamps, and chairs decorated by the artists for their dealers.

Influential dealers in other art neighborhoods regarded the East Village scene as one filled with youthful energy and talent. Its dealers opened their galleries here in small, low-rent spaces in the early 1980s to give starving, talented artists a chance to show their works and make dynamic, fresh statements in the art world. The experiment worked. The most important art critics in the world paid attention to the East Village scene. Within less than a decade, the artists and the gallery dealers acted as a pioneering cultural and architectural force in the East Village, reclaiming abandoned and decaying buildings for their community, convincing landlords to follow suit, and causing such gentrification that the East Village has become an attractive, safe, and inevitably, an expensive place to live. In fact, by 1988 rents in the East Village had risen above those for large gallery spaces on Broadway between Houston and Canal streets, within the Soho neighborhood. As a result, the East Village galleries began to move en masse to amalgamate the city's art scene within Soho's sphere.

Lower East Side and the East Village

By the end of 1989, little will remain of the East Village art galleries. Outdoor wall graffiti by Chico at such sites as Tompkins Square Park at 10th Street and Avenue B will testify to the scene's former vitality for as long as the weather leaves the paint intact.

Chinatown History Project, which is publicly funded, offers the most comprehensive tour of Chinatown. The directors have a highly regarded research library at their disposal for resource material. Located in the heart of Chinatown, at 70 Mulberry Street, on the second floor of a former public-school building, the project sponsors a twenty-five-minute slide show on the history of Chinatown, followed by a sixty-minute walk to bridge the information gap between the burgeoning Chinese community and the rest of American society. (Usually the show-and-walk takes place twice daily, at 11:00 A.M. and 2:00 P.M. But call the project to confirm the schedule.) "Charlie" Chin, the project's tour coordinator, narrates the show and then leads groups through the Chinatown streets, which he knows thoroughly.

The project's office has such daffy touches as an old "Hand Laundry" sign and other emblems from Chinese-American businesses hung as pop art. In the project's reference library, a resource for works on Chinese socioeconomic history in the United States, Mr. Chin flips the switch for the engrossing slide show. And his deep, professional, broadcast-style voice narrates the show on tape.

Beginning with artists' sketches, the show traces Chinatown's history through the early Indian, Dutch, and English settlements to a community of black freemen who worked for abolition. They were pushed uptown to Greenwich Village in the mid-nineteenth century, when Irish and German immigrants fleeing war and famine in Europe arrived to dominate the poor neighborhood that would become Chinatown. Its pond became polluted by butchers and tanners, posing a dire health hazard. The pond basin was eventually filled in, and houses for immigrants were built atop it. The connector to the Hudson River was paved and called Canal Street.

Another wave of immigrants, Italians and Jews, moved into the neighborhood, rich in culture, poor in worldly goods. Italianate details still embellish some Chinatown buildings. Mr. Chin makes sure tourists see the cornices carved by the talented Italian stonecarvers as well as the area's "back buildings" placed on alleys. They were erected behind buildings facing streets, so that landlords could collect additional rents from poor immigrants.

The first Chinese settler arrived in the 1840s—an atypical export-import tea dealer who was always in trouble with the law. By the 1870s, the Chinese began arriving in greater numbers. They came from Canton through Hong Kong to help build railroads in the United States, but, persecuted in the Midwest, they fled to the East and West coasts. By 1900 a small, hardy community established itself in New York City and called itself the Bachelor Society (few women had come with the workers from China). Furthermore, in the 1880s Congress had passed a law prohibiting most Chinese, with the exception of students, teachers, and merchants, from entering the United States. These men opened self-help community groups, service businesses, stores, restaurants, and weekend gambling games to band together. A few intermarried with white women; a few had Chinese wives. Altogether there were only eighty-four married couples—thirty-six men with Chinese wives, the rest with white wives—in Chinatown by 1898.

After the slide show Chin, who was born in Queens and lived for a while in Chinatown, takes groups on an insider's walk. When he was growing up, he recalls, Americans were falling increasingly in love with Chinese cuisine in the thriving Mott, Doyers, and Pell street restaurants: Chinatown's nucleus.

Long, narrow Doyers Street, with several twists and turns, was once a popular place for assassinations to settle gambling debts. Killers made quick exits out of Doyers through Pell or the Bowery or through an arcade that once cut from Doyers to Mott.

Mr. Chin points out the corner of Pell and Doyers streets, where, at the turn of the century, someone shot at an infamous Chinese gambler, Mock Dock. But his lucky silver-dollar belt buckle deflected the bullet. After that, Mock Dock, whose high-living ways earned him the English nickname "Kid Dropper," showed off his dented buckle proudly.

On Doyers, too, Mr. Chin draws tourists' attention to the old-fashioned, red-and-white-striped "candycane" barbershop poles still standing here. Chinese men used to—and still do—frequent the parlors to spruce themselves up.

Mr. Chin also points out the eye-catching carvings of two carps atop a building embellished with pagoda-style details, now the North Garden Seafood Restaurant, 24 Pell Street. Good-luck symbols, the carps are poised to fly away into the sky. The building may be torn down in the foreseeable future, Mr. Chin opines with sadness, because Chinese immigrants require more space in high-rise buildings for apartments and businesses. (Chinatown's buildings don't have landmark designation to protect them from demolition.)

Another symbol of Chinatown's past is the chinaware shop, Quong Yuen Shing, at 32 Mott Street, owned by the Lee family since 1891. Other chinaware shops have been renovated through the years, but the Lee family has kept the old decor, including a sumptuous wall full of ornate, hand-carved wooden paneling.

A sign of the new times in Chinatown stands at the corner of Canal and Mott streets. The building, with a bank on the ground floor, is headquarters for Maria's, a chain of popular bakeries in Chinatown. Maria's puts colorful decorations on frilly, French-looking pastries in its shops, which are scattered around the community. The new, big-city immigrants, who are far more sophisticated than their pioneering, country-born predecessors, like European-style cakes. In the Maria's branch on Lafayette Street, one block north of Canal, a pretty clerk recently told a tourist the name of one cake in Chinese. And a bevy of Chinese clerks gathered around to giggle, smile, and ponder about translations. Maria's decor in that store is straight out of McDonald's. On Canal Street, another Maria's shop looks like a Parisian *patisserie*.

Justin Ferate leads a tour of Little Italy and Irish New York, pointing out traces of what he calls "Little Ireland" within Little Italy. Old St. Patrick's Cathedral, between parallel Mott and Mulberry streets, and Prince and East Houston streets, is still used as a church. And people can still be buried in the catacombs downstairs, if they have vault rights. (The tour visits the catacombs.)

Ferate leads another tour of the Lower East Side, to point out the layers of history within Chinatown, such as the old Portuguese-Spanish Sephardic cemetery on St. James Place near Chatham Square. Oliver Street nearby was also within Irish New York's boundaries.

Marvin Gelfand's Walk of the Town goes to the Lower East Side for a tour that can range from two to four hours. Gelfand, who calls himself "a village explainer," takes people on a round of old synagogues, including the Eldridge Street Synagogue (now called the Eldridge Street Project, because it is being renovated). Though in colossal disrepair, the synagogue's interior still has magnificent details. The men used to sit on a raised platform in the center of the synagogue to lead the services, while the women had separate sections in the gallery, or balcony, according to Orthodox Jewish law.

Gelfand also leads groups to the *Daily Forward* Building on East Broadway, which once housed the influential Yiddish-language newspaper. Nobel prize winner Isaac Bashevis Singer wrote many of his great stories in Yiddish for this paper. A Chinese self-help group now operates in the building. Gelfand stands in front of it and talks about the great editors and writers who once worked there and the intellectual ferment of their heyday.

He walks to the Educational Alliance, an old settlement house on East Broadway, where immigrant children used to find refuge. The Alliance sent many of them to summer camp in the country. Photographs of some of those children, who grew up to become famous—for example, old-time comedian Eddie Cantor—now hang in a small exhibit area off the lobby. Gelfand also visits the Henry Street Settlement House, where he talks about Lillian Wald, the German-Jewish nurse who founded the Settlement House to help Italian and Jewish immigrants adjust to the New World. Gelfand's detailed descriptions of the neighborhood—for example, the fights between anarchists and socialists—make the social, cultural, and political forces of the late nineteenth century come alive. The tour ends on Essex Street, where

Gelfand points out historic shops. "Usually I lose people to the pickle man," says Gelfand, "or else to a bakery." Once a commercial center for the Jewish community, Essex Street used to have lines of pushcarts. Louis Stavisky's bookstore, which specializes in books on Jewish subjects for adults and children, still exists. And Gelfand points the way to Schapiro's, a kosher winery and the only wine maker in town, as well as to the Streit Matzoth Co., east of Schapiro's on Rivington Street.

Letha Hadadi, who spent years studying acupuncture and herbology, a 2,000-year-old medical tradition, in China, begins her walking tours, under the aegis of the New York Open Center, with a lecture. She introduces people to the concepts of Chinese medicine, and she talks about the values of certain foods and herbs as tonics, as well as medicines, for all types of maladies and physical discomforts, from headaches to liver diseases and constipation.

After this introduction to the principles of Chinese medicine, Ms. Hadadi leads her groups to some of the scores of herbal shops in Chinatown to see their herbal medicine counters or, in some cases, whole shops filled with various over-the-counter medicines or herbs.

Jeffrey Kroessler's Lower East Side tour crosses the borders of several neighborhoods. Mr. Kroessler begins his only Manhattan tour at City Hall and walks through City Hall Park to get to the Tweed Courthouse, at 52 Chambers Street, between Broadway and Centre streets. Built in the 1870s, it was known not only as the Criminal Court of New York City but as a monument to some of the city's most persistent political institutions: Tammany Hall and the Tweed Ring. Corrupt politicians discerned that the immigrants were a source of votes that could be bought with jobs. Once the politicians took office, they could also make money by working with contractors to pad the bills for city contracts. This courthouse eventually cost four times its projected budget—and still isn't finished; it lacks its planned dome. The Tweed Ring, which ran Tammany Hall and controlled city government, with nationwide repercussions, made $10 million on the courthouse's $14 million cost. In the 1940s the city removed the steps leading to the building's Corinthian portico; visitors must enter the building through its basement. Though in disrepair, the courthouse has an excellent Anglo-Italian exterior.

Kroessler also visits the Municipal Building on Centre Street, straddling Chambers Street, built in 1913 by the famous architectural firm of McKim, Mead and White. The Municipal Building was meant to handle the additional paperwork generated by the incorporation of the boroughs of Bronx, Queens, Staten Island, and Brooklyn into New York City. The building had to provide a huge amount of floor space on an oddly shaped site without overwhelming nearby City Hall. The result is a structure in the form of a lopsided U with a Corinthian colonnade joining the two wings. And this large, imposing, highly decorated building is topped by a ten-story colonnaded tower, and a twenty-five-foot statue of "Civic Fame" among many other elaborations—"a classic stew," as tour leader John Tauranac described the building.

From there Kroessler continues north to the neighborhood once known as Five Points. It began its residential history as a neighborhood for Irish immigrants. They were crammed into housing atop a landfill in the nineteenth century. Five Points no longer exists, but in its heyday, in the late nineteenth century, just below Chinatown's center, Five Points became infamous as a haven for criminals of every type. On one of its streets, a staggering number of murders took place. Jacob Riis, European-born photojournalist, wrote about Five Points in such graphic detail that he triggered a cleanup of the area. Columbus Park at the southern tip of Chinatown was built to replace part of Five Points, which was torn down. Kroessler's tour passes through Chinatown and ends at the Oliver Street house in Irish New York where Governor Al Smith of New York grew up.

Karen Lee, a Chinese cooking teacher and an author of books on Chinese cuisine, leads occasional early-morning tours, on Sundays, to Chinatown's food shops and stalls. Beginning at a food shop on the Little Italy side of Canal Street, Lee inadvertently shows you how Chinatown has pushed beyond its traditional borders and has turned Little Italy into a frieze of Chinese signs. Lee guides you to the right vegetables at the right time of year. She chooses to go shopping early on Sunday mornings, she says, because that's when the Chinese themselves do their shopping for the coming week, and the food is always fresh then. So you join the Chinese as they immerse themselves in one of their most important cultural exploits—food shopping.

Michael Levin devotes several Sunday afternoons, in his walking-tour season, to "East Village History," beginning with the development of the area as Dutch Governor Peter Stuyvesant's *bouwerie* in the seventeenth century. The lecture progresses all the way to Andy Warhol's influence on the art and mores of the East Village in the mid-twentieth century. The entire tour takes place within a three-and-one-half-block area, with a lecture as condensed and refreshing as the contents of a Campbell Soup can. Traces of the beatniks, whose "guru" was poet Allen Ginsburg, can be found in the neighborhood, too. Ginsburg moved into an E. 7th Street apartment in the 1950s.

Barry Lewis leads a walk through Chinatown and Little Italy, stressing their nineteenth-century role as middle-class, ethnic neighborhoods. The mix of nineteenth-century townhouses and late nineteenth-century-early twentieth-century tenements fascinates Mr. Lewis, who embroiders upon the life-styles of tenement residents and talks about the new- and old-law tenements. (New laws governing tenement construction were intended to improve the safety of the buildings.)

The Municipal Art Society sponsors a Jewish Lower East Side tour, engaging Betty Sandler, a lifelong resident of the neighborhood, as guide. Sandler works for the Eldridge Street Project, which is restoring the Eldridge Street Synagogue, built in the 1880s.

She begins at this synagogue, discussing its architecture and history, showing off its pretty, period interior, and ends the walk several hours later at the Bialystoker Synagogue on Willett Street.

In between those points, she heads for the Pike Street Synagogue, which has obviously been neglected and vandalized, and then, walking east, passes old Society buildings that once helped the Eastern European Jewish immigrants adapt to life in the United States. She calls attention to a Chinese restaurant that, until recent years, was the Garden Cafeteria, a popular place with Jewish immigrants, including Nobel Prize-winning writer Isaac Bashevis Singer. The tour moves to the *Daily Forward* Building nearby and progresses to the Seward Park Library, built in the early years of the twentieth century.

Ms. Sandler talks about the park movement on the Lower East Side, which gave children a place to play out of the street. She visits the Educational Alliance Building, which began the park movement and provided summer-camp vacations for children. She continually points out intriguing details: for example, a building with Jewish stars built right into its facade on East Broadway near the *Daily Forward* Building. A similar building, which is being converted to a condominium, stands on Orchard Street off Canal. The buildings' owners included the stars to signal to Jews that they were welcome there. The architects were the Herter Brothers (Francis and Peter), of non-Jewish, German background; they also built the Eldridge Street Synagogue.

About 100 old storefront synagogues still exist in the neighborhood. Their congregations rent and share space, because they can't afford to build individual synagogues. The religion of these groups is Orthodox Judaism, but each group takes its identity from its neighborhood of origin in Eastern Europe.

The tour also goes to Grand Street and the Henry Street Settlement House, with its new building for the arts, the Louis Abrons Arts for Living Center.

Ms. Sandler also points out the turn-of-the-century Arnold Toynbee Hall, originally a settlement center, which became a *mikvah,* or ritual bathhouse for Orthodox Jewish women, and still functions as one today.

Ms. Sandler leads tours by special request. The Educational Alliance and the United Jewish Council sponsor Lower East Side tours on a more regular basis. For information, call the Eldridge Street Project, 219–0888; the Educational Alliance, 475–6200; or the United Jewish Council, 233–6037.

The **Museum of the City of New York** schedules a tour led by Hope Cooke, administrator of the museum's tour program since 1987, entitled

Lower East Side and the East Village

"Two Centuries Plus on the Lower East Side." This tour focuses on the spiritual, economic, and social history of the Lower East Side, beginning with a discussion of the original Delancey and Rutgers estates here, continuing to the shipbuilding period, on to the Irish settlement and the Russian-Jewish immigrants, to the current Hispanic and Chinese communities. The tour starts in Chinatown—in 1988 at the front door of the Wing Shing Restaurant on Seward Square at East Broadway and Rutgers Street—once a quintessentially Jewish neighborhood.

"Irish Life in Early New York" is another Museum of the City of New York tour of this sprawling conglomeration of neighborhoods called the Lower East Side. The tour, a new one in 1988, starts at the Broadway entrance of St. Paul's Chapel on Fulton Street and Broadway, in the historic district, and travels up to the Five Points neighborhood north of City Hall and on to Old St. Patrick's Cathedral, built in 1815. The tour lecture is filled with legend, lore, and history of prominent Irish-Americans from the Revolutionary era to the Civil War and beyond.

The New-York Historical Society conducts a tour that begins at St. Mark's-in-the-Bowery on Second Avenue and 10th Street, a historic Georgian church, built on the site of Dutch Governor Peter Stuyvesant's private *bouwerie* house. The tour then moves a bit southwest, to the site where architect Stanford White was born on 10th Street. To the right stands Renwick Triangle—a group of sixteen quaint landmark townhouses—one of New York's gemlike communities, built in 1861 by renowned architect James Renwick, Jr.

From there, the walk goes south to St. Mark's Place, now a headquarters for the counterculture. A low-rent district for decades, in the midst of an ethnic neighborhood, St. Mark's Place now boasts some expensive cooperative apartments in fancifully renovated walk-up tenements. The tour continues to Cooper Square for a discussion of Cooper Union, founded in 1859 as the first free educational institution in New York. Around the corner on Lafayette Street, the tour finds the Public Theater across the street from Colonnade Row, named for its series of marble, Corinthian columns. Farther along, the group stops to visit the Old Merchant's House at 29 E. 4th Street, built in the 1830s for a prosperous merchant. The house still retains some of its exterior and interior decorations and period-style furniture. The southernmost point of the tour is the Puck Building, a large, prepossessing landmark at the corner of East Houston and Lafayette streets, once a publishing headquarters nicknamed for the figure of Puck on its facade. Today the building is used by cultural and civic groups, businesses, and even for parties attended by the socially prominent, who enter under floodlights with flashbulbs popping around them. The tour returns to Cooper Union for drinks and hors d'oeuvres.

New York Walkabout, a private tour firm, schedules a walk through Chinatown and Little Italy called "Ethnic Contrasts," which compares these enclaves to Hong Kong and Naples. The firm also schedules a completely different tour of the Lower East Side's northern reaches—Astor Place and the East Village—calling the walk "The Old and the New." Using the Public Theater as a centerpiece, the lecture traces the history of the neighborhood, from the founding of the John Jacob Astor Library in the mid-nineteenth century to the current vital scene of experimental theaters and artists' lofts. They are turning the neighborhood into a fashionable district again, after 150 years of ups and downs in fortune and men's eyes.

A third New York Walkabout tour of the Lower East Side, "Home of Immigrants," begins at the southwest corner of Chrystie and Grand streets and looks for traces of the German and Irish migrations.

The Germans fled war in Europe; the Irish escaped famine. Eventually they moved uptown and were replaced by Jewish refugees from Eastern Europe. All the firm's tours have morning and afternoon sessions on their scheduled days.

The **92nd Street "Y"** has several Lower East Side walking tours in its repertoire. One is in the East Village and focuses on an area that figured in early American history: the territory of the old *bouwerie*, or homestead, of the first Dutch Governor, Peter Stuyvesant. (The Dutch word was later used for the street now called the Bowery.) Peter Stuyvesant was buried on the land of St. Mark's Church in the Bowery on Second

Avenue at 10th Street, near Stuyvesant Place. The tour also goes to Cooper Union and the Old Merchant's House, while the tour leader recounts the development of the area from farmland to a wealthy enclave, to an immigrant neighborhood, to a counterculture center, art district, and ethnic stronghold.

The "Y" also sponsors a tour called "A Day in Irish New York," led by Columbia University history professor, James Shenton, who visits the remaining Irish churches and institutions, including Old St. Patrick's and its catacombs. Finally, the "Y" also regularly offers tours of artists' studios. Sculptor Debra Chase's East Village studio was the focus of the 1988 tour, and several other neighborhood artists joined Ms. Chase in opening their studios to public view. Ms. Chase's aluminum constructions have been shown in galleries and used as decorations in the headquarters of international companies.

Note: The "Y's" specific tours vary from year to year, so check with the "Y" for its itineraries each season. The neighborhoods visited may remain essentially the same, but the vantage points may change.

The **Park Rangers** occasionally lead groups into little neighborhood parks such as Columbus Park, dating back to 1897, on Chinatown's southern border. The park was created to clean up a notoriously seamy area called Five Points. Recently, the Chinese painted the park house bright red with a gold dragon and other lucky symbols as decorations emblematic of the Chinese reign in the neighborhood. The tour is free.

Rosa Ross, a Chinese cooking-school teacher, leads tour of Chinatown on weekend mornings, beginning with a lecture to her students and any members of the public who join. She's a chatty fount of knowledge and insight into Chinese culture, telling you tidbits such as the following: Herbal medicines are used as tonics over a long period of time, not as the main medicines to cure illnesses. The tonics are packaged as prettily as French perfumes and often cost as much. Ms. Ross also tells you that Chinese pastry shops decorate some cookies with bright icings to Westernize and differentiate them from the plain-looking, traditional Chinese sweets. And she explains, amidst peals of her own laughter, that the

Chinese culture is very food-oriented, because the Chinese believe that life's greatest pleasures are food and sex. "And food lasts longer," she says.

Her tour officially begins with a dim sum meal, which originated as the background for business negotiations in China. This meal consists of tea accompanied by a great variety of tempting snacks—duck, chicken, fish, shrimp, and potato bits, fried, boiled, and sauteed. The dim sum custom has been gaining steadily in popularity in American Chinatowns in recent years. The Silver Palace, a cavernous upstairs restaurant on the Bowery near Canal Street, has long been famous for its daily dim sum, served from 8:00 A.M. to 4:00 A.M. Ms. Ross has taken groups there and to other restaurants.

After dim sum, Ms. Ross leads groups to shop at outdoor vendor stands and indoor grocery stores. She explains what the vegetables are, how to cook them, and what herbs and spices to use. She tells you, for example, to store the rare pink-stemmed ginger (and all ginger) in sherry in the refrigerator. She describes how to cook "long beans," which are as long as spaghetti and as hard as carrots, with ginger to bring out the flavor. And she explains that duck eggs are kept in brine for a month and eaten as hard-boiled eggs.

That's the essence of her tour. But along the way, she points out the economical Southeast Asian restaurants and shops. She likes the Lung Moon Bakery, 83 Mulberry, for Chinese cakes, cookies, and patties with fillings ranging from black beans to beef and pork. Her own favorite grocery is the Chinese-American Trading Company on Mulberry Street near Canal Street. Chinese-cuisine fanciers will find bags of shiny, dried silverfish and anchovies among the thousands of items there.

"The fish make the whole house smell when you cook them," advises Ms. Ross. The higher-priced Kam Man grocery at 200 Canal Street is interesting, too, filled with herbal medicine, groceries, and housewares. Mobs wait to pay at the cash registers in both groceries.

Walking along Mott Street, Ms. Ross tosses out a great deal of information printed nowhere. And all the while, you notice the hubbub on the street.

New immigrants rent sidewalk space at high fees from established store owners. Rents for space here are climbing toward the city's highest levels. Outside a jewelry store, you find a clothing and electronics vendor. Outside a vegetable store, fishmongers spread out huge red snappers with crimson-colored jaws, neat little butterfish, and wiggling crabs with rainbow-colored claws. And a few steps away, you'll find the opposite situation. On Mulberry near Canal Street, you'll find a vegetable vendor outside a fish store. Some days, the tanks inside and in the windows swarm with fish of all types, their mouths working the water for oxygen, their bodies vying for space. And in a wall-tank inside, the Chinese, who originally bred goldfish, keep a stock of them. Their ranks thin out during the Chinese New Year in late winter: because their gold color is considered a good-luck omen, they're given as gifts to children.

Growing numbers of grocery stores sell produce from all over Southeast Asia (such as *confiture de Durian* from Malaysia, a jelly made from a yellow fruit encased in what looks, in the picture on the side of the can, like a pine cone. The jelly tastes like ultra-sweet apricot). Wing Woh grocery on the corner of Mott and Bayard streets has a big inventory of Southeast Asian goods to accommodate the ethnic Chinese who have migrated here from all over Southeast Asia.

Ms. Ross points out restaurants and stores popular with the Chinese, such as the antique store, Tai Hung Lee, Inc., at 60-A Mott Street, where you can pay several hundred dollars for a vase. "That's one of the few places where it's not all junk," says Ms. Ross. "That's a very good place."

She bypasses the Eastern States Buddhist Temple of America on Mott between Bayard and Canal streets, where the fortunes for sale are less pungent than the ones in fortune cookies and cost fifty cents. But you can light an incense stick and kneel before Buddha in a calm little storefront temple, alongside many Asians. There are more than a dozen Buddhist temples and Christian churches in Chinatown, most of whose inhabitants subscribe to these major religions and to Confucianism, a code of ethics, and Taoism, a collection of philosophies and folk myths— all reflecting the religious composition of China.

Joseph L. Schiff, among his many tours of current and former Jewish neighborhoods, in his "Jewish Urban Study Tours" repertoire, calls his Lower East Side tour "World of Our Fathers." He concentrates on the era of immigration from 1880 to 1920, when the Yiddish press, theater, and synagogues flourished. Many traces of Jewish cultural life remain, including Stars of David built into building facades, though many of the old cultural institutions have been taken over by Hispanic and Chinese immigrants.

Professor James Shenton leads a tour of Irish New York for the 92nd Street "Y" and also for Columbia University's "Encore" series. The walk begins at City Hall and continues northward to St. Peter's Church; the Five Points area at the southern tip of Chinatown, the heart of the mid-nineteenth-century Irish ghetto; St. James's Roman Catholic Church, the home parish of New York Governor Al Smith; and Boss Tweed's headquarters. The tour ends with a visit to Old St. Patrick Cathedral's catacombs.

Professor Shenton also leads a tour of "Jewish Life on the Lower East Side," beginning at Chatham Square, now in the center of Chinatown. He goes into St. James Place's seventeenth-century Sephardic cemetery, which belongs to the Congregation She'arith Israel, now on the Upper West Side, and continues to the Eldridge Street Synagogue, built in the 1880s by Russian Jews. It was once the largest synagogue on the Lower East Side. The tour takes in Straus Square and the *Daily Forward* Building, turns into Hester Street for a treat at Gertel's Bakery, and continues into Grand Street to visit kosher food shops, ending at Schapiro's Winery on Rivington Street.

Professor Shenton also conducts a tour of "Chinatown and Little Italy" beginning at Confucius Towers, just north of exotic Chatham Square with its bright red-and-gold pagoda-style bank. Shenton shows how Chinatown has moved across the Bowery and up East Broadway and sprawled into the former Jewish enclave; he takes groups through the Mott, Pell, and Doyers streets enclave, which formed the nucleus of Chinatown beginning in the mid-nineteenth century until the 1960s, and stops in the Chinatown Historical Society and the Family Associations Building, the latter housing an organization that is a particularly influential force in the enclave. Surrounded by food shops and restaurants, Professor Shenton points out the new and the old, then crosses Canal Street, once Chinatown's northern border, into Little Italy.

105

Chinatown's growth has encroached upon Little Italy, whose population is dwindling. Shenton provides a close look at this boomtown within a city. Dr. Peter Kwong, Associate Professor at the State University of New York in Old Westbury, Long Island, and an author of books about New York's Chinatown, before and after Congress lifted the Chinese Exclusion Act, assists Dr. Shenton in explaining that new immigrants are coming from Hong Kong, because the British lease on the colony will run out by 1997. Hong Kong businessmen are transferring their companies for security in advance of the deadline. Other Hong Kong Chinese and Southeast Asia's ethnic Chinese populations want to establish themselves in the United States in any case for similar reasons.

In Little Italy, Shenton tours Mulberry and a few other streets in the heart of the old ethnic neighborhood, which dates back to the late nineteenth century. He shows how these streets have become a gentrified tourist attraction—a great place for rich and tasty meals and desserts. He also points out the area's architectural highlights and sheds light on the social, economic, and political forces that brought Little Italy into being and kept it a tightly knit community for decades. Essentially, he notes, "Little Italy is a pleasant place to pretend that you're in Italy, but not too much."

Jeff Sholeen, who emphasizes neighborhood architecture, likes to begin a tour of St. Mark's Church in the Bowery, from which he ambles around the area just below Cooper Square. Between Broadway and Lafayette streets, at 55 Bleecker Street, he stops to examine the Bayard Building, designed by the well-known nineteenth-century architect, Louis Sullivan. He also points out the building standing on the northeast corner of Broadway at Bond Street, which was the Brooks Brothers store from 1874 to 1884. And, of course, he talks about the Public Theater on Lafayette Street, discussing its history as the Astor Library and the status of the buildings across the street, known as Colonnade Row. He then makes his way up to Grace Church at Broadway and 10th Street, where the tour ends.

Lou Singer, a Brooklyn specialist, ventures into lower Manhattan for two hours of the ethnic roots of Eastern European Jews. He begins one tour, "The Lower East Side Tour and Lunch," in the Second Avenue Deli at 10th Street. Regarded as one of the best delis and one of the few kosher delicatessens in New York, the Second Avenue Deli has won kudos for its matzo balls in a local media poll. It sets the tone for the Singer tour, which then provides a minibus to take the group southward on the Lower East Side to the neighborhood of the *Daily Forward* Building, where the Yiddish newspaper used to publish regularly.

From there, the tour proceeds to various shops, where tour members can browse for books on Jewish subjects, objets d'art, and religious articles, and then goes to Gertel's, a pastry shop at 53 Hester Street for *rugalach, hamentaschen, babka,* and *challah*—typical Eastern European and Jewish pastries and breads. The next stop is Schapiro's Winery and its wine-tasting facilities, at 126 Rivington Street, between Essex and Norfolk streets. The only winery in town, it has free wine-tastings open to the the public every Sunday; however, it's suggested that you buy a bottle of wine as the price of the tour. (Bottles begin at about $2.) As part of Singer's tour, the winery admits his groups on weekdays, too. (Call 475–7383 if you would like to tour the winery on your own.) From there, the tour goes to a century-old Romanian synagogue, where the rabbi delivers a lecture about the synagogue's past glories and present neediness. Listeners are thereby effectively asked to make a donation. The tour begins at lunchtime and ends at about 4:00 P.M.

Singer's other Lower East Side tour, called "Noshing in New York," has gotten a great deal of publicity. "Noshing in New York" visits restaurants serving all types of ethnic specialties, from cannoli to knishes to pierogi to dim sum. The tour ends at the Second Avenue Deli. What you cannot eat, you're encouraged to wrap up in little packages and take home.

John Tauranac's East Village tour starts at Cooper Union, on Astor Place, at 8th Street between Third and Fourth avenues, and walks east on St. Mark's Place, a continuation of 8th Street. From Second Avenue, Tauranac heads west on 7th Street to look at McSorley's Old Ale House, which claims to be the oldest bar operating exclusively as such in New York City. (Pete's Tavern, a restaurant in the Gramercy Park neighborhood, has a bar that is even older.) From McSorley's, which didn't admit women until the women's movement in the 1970s, Tauranac heads west to Cooper Union's Great Hall, between Third Avenue and the Bowery, and walks west for another block to Lafayette Street's Colonnade Row. John Jacob Astor provided an endowment of $400,000 to start New York City's first public library there. Now it houses the Public Theater, run by the brilliant theatrical entrepreneur Joseph Papp. After the library moved, the building housed the Hebrew Immigrant Aid Society for a while, then was slated for demolition. Papp saved it when he bought and converted it to off-Broadway theater spaces.

The tour continues to Bond Street, where Albert Gallatin, President Jefferson's Secretary of the Treasury, lived on the site of No. 1. Then Tauranac leads the way to the Old Merchant's House, at 29 E. 4th Street, between Lafayette Street and the Bowery—an intact, early-nineteenth-century landmark Federal-style house, with a hint of Greek Revival in the Ionic columns near the door. In 1935 a nonprofit corporation bought and restored it. Now, on Sundays or by appointment, for a small fee, the house is open for public tours. Call 777–1089 for the schedule.

The last stops on the tour are the Romanesque Revival-style DeVinne Press Building, erected for office space and printing presses; the Havemeyer Building on Lafayette Street, built with money from a sugar fortune; and a historic firehouse at 44 Great Jones Street. Tauranac sometimes leads this tour under the auspices of the Municipal Art Society, with its architectural and city planning orientation.

Gerard Wolfe, a well-known city historian, leads a tour called "Lower East Side pre-Passover Tour" under the auspices of the 92nd Street "Y." The walk takes place on the Sunday before the Jewish Passover holiday. Wolfe gives a detailed history of the Lower East Side's former Jewish enclave, pointing out the sites of tenements, sweatshops, and institutions, including the 1887 Eldridge Street synagogue, formally called Congregation Adath Jeshurun, at 14 Eldridge Street, between Canal and Forsyth streets. With its rose window and Moorish decorations, which are still intact, the synagogue was once the largest and most important in a neighborhood with about 500 synagogues. Nowadays, however, the synagogue, which is not used, shows the effects of neglect and vandalism during the past fifty years.

Note: Marvin Gelfand and Val Ginter, of Walk of the Town and Ginter-Gotham Urban History, respectively, created a four-day tour of the Lower East Side to present to an international conference. Both tour leaders will re-create the tour on request, visiting the Second Avenue Yiddish Theater neighborhood, with lunch at Katz's Delicatessen on E. Houston Street, and a walk around the Lower East Side.

Chapter Six

Lower Midtown Manhattan:
Ladies' Mile, Gramercy Park, Chelsea, Madison Square, and Murray Hill

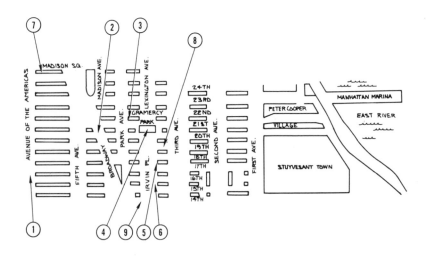

Points of Interest in Ladies' Mile, Gramercy Park, and Madison Square

1. Sixth Avenue
2. Broadway
3. Calvary Church
4. Gramercy Park
5. Pete's Tavern

6. Irving Place
7. Serbian Orthodox Church of St. Sava
8. "The Block Beautiful"
9. Former Luchow's Restaurant building

To this day, these lower midtown neighborhoods reflect society on the march. In the nineteenth century they were thriving centers for wealthy, socially prominent New Yorkers. By World War I, they had gone into eclipse in varying ways. But in the 1970s, and especially the '80s, New Yorkers in search of affordable space began renovating and rejuvenating this section of town.

For example, in the early nineteenth century, Union Square was a lively place, full of children from affluent neighborhood families and their nannies. The neighborhood became the hub of an elegant shopping center after the Civil War. By the early twentieth century it had metamorphosed even further into a place for political groups to air their views. And by mid-century, it fell into disrepute as a haven for oddballs, addicts, and criminals. By the 1980s, almost miraculously, it would seem, it was a fashionable place again. Union Square Park now serves as the centerpiece of a newly chic neighborhood. On its borders are new luxury apartment houses, from which affluent families now take their children to play in the park. On the west and north, a colorful farmers' market attracts shoppers in droves on Wednesdays, Fridays, and Saturdays. And a new statue of Gandhi stands in the square's southeast corner.

Another example of a neighborhood starting to come full-circle is Ladies' Mile, just above the park. In the nineteenth century, Ladies' Mile boasted bigger and better department stores than New York had ever seen before. The neighborhood fell out of vogue in the early twentieth century, when these stores moved uptown. In recent years, however, fine publishing houses and photographic agencies and studios have been filtering in and settling into the excellent, sturdy old stone buildings on and near Broadway, between Union Square at 14th Street and Madison Square beginning at 23rd Street. And the neighborhood seems to be starting a mini-renaissance. What the buildings need most is a cleaning to show off how striking they still are.

Not everybody offers tours of these areas. But they fascinate some guides, who regard them as a treasure trove of things to look at and talk about; sometimes the guides cross lines from one neighborhood to another in a single tour.

Here is a brief history of the heyday of this neighborhood:

From the Civil War era until the turn of the century, some of the city's great department stores and hotels moved uptown or opened on a stretch of Broadway beginning at 10th Street, near Grace (Episcopal) Church, and ending at 23rd Street, near Madison Square. Since fashionable women went shopping on this strip, it was dubbed Ladies' Mile. Sixth Avenue, too, had several fine stores, included in Ladies' Mile. As luck would have it, nobody ever bothered to tear down the buildings after the stores moved farther uptown in the twentieth century, so the view up Broadway from Union Square or down from 23rd Street hasn't changed much architecturally in the last 100 years.

Nearby, an enterprising lawyer and real estate developer named Samuel Ruggles had the bright idea to create an urban neighborhood around a private park. In 1831 he drained a parcel of swampy land that became Gramercy Park, protected by high gates and modeled on the traditional English plan of placing a garden in a square. Single families lived in the varied, architecturally distinguished, nineteenth-century houses around the park—including two Gothic brownstones built in the 1850s. Later they were joined together as a residence for New York

Governor Samuel Tilden; now they serve as the National Arts Club at 15 Gramercy Park South.

When the neighborhood first developed, each family who lived around the park had a key to the gate. The key system still exists, but now hundreds of keys are rented to the people who live around Gramercy Park, in the old, private houses that were converted to apartments. Keys rent for $175 from the Gramercy Neighborhood Associates, Inc., a group active in preserving the cachet of the neighborhood and in trying to get landmark designation for nearby Ladies' Mile.

In the mid-nineteenth century, Shakespearean actor Edwin Booth numbered among the park's neighbors. With the help of several other prominent actors—including John Drew of the Barrymore-Drew dynasty and comedic actor Joseph Jefferson—writer Mark Twain, and even General William Tecumseh Sherman, Booth founded the Players Club at 16 Gramercy Park South, which celebrated its 100th anniversary in 1988 (the same year it started to admit women members). The purpose of the club was to promote the social status of actors, who weren't considered quite respectable in conservative society in those days. In the 1880s, too, the first apartments opened on Gramercy Park's fringes. Socially prominent residents in private houses were affronted; they thought the risqué living arrangement, with living rooms next to bedrooms, would lead to the destruction of family life. Some of them must have been alarmed at the type of people moving into the apartments, too. O. Henry, the short story writer and newspaperman, lived in an Irving Place rooming house from 1902 to 1910. Now a cheerful Italian restaurant, Sal Anthony's, it has a plaque on the door commemorating O. Henry's residence there, where he wrote his sentimental story, "The Gift of the Magi." O. Henry used to go across the street with a friend from the *New York World* newspaper and drink in Pete's Tavern, an Italian restaurant, on Irving Place and 18th Street. The restaurant dates back to 1864, when it was called Healey's. (The building is about 20 years older than that, and because it has had a bar for 124 years, it vies with McSorley's Old Ale House on E. 7th Street for the honor of calling itself the city's oldest bar.) Pete's also claims that O. Henry wrote there.

As various *artistes* gave the neighborhood a new kind of cachet, the upper middle-class moved uptown, leaving Gramercy Park to become a neighborhood of rooming houses by the 1920s. Along came the Depression, followed by World War II, to discourage its development. Afterward, builders had little interest in Gramercy Park, with tenements standing only a few blocks to the south, on 14th Street. It wouldn't be profitable for developers to put up high-rises here, they decided, when people wanted to live on the Upper East Side. So the wreckers' ball bypassed Gramercy Park.

Then, in the 1960s, people noticed how beautiful the old houses were. The city declared Gramercy Park a landmark, protected by law from demolition. In 1988 a four-story townhouse near the National Arts Club was reportedly sold for $1.5 million, and a doctor bought two two-bedroom apartments in his building in the Park's vicinity at the *insider's* price of $200,000 apiece. If apartments stand within five blocks of the historic landmark district, owners give them élan by advertising them as "near Gramercy Park."

The district cuts a wiggly swath over a six-block area plus the core park, excluding the Gramercy Park Hotel on the park's fringe (the hotel replaced Stanford White's private house there about sixty years ago) but including Pete's Tavern and several other nineteenth-century buildings. Among them, usually pointed out by all the guides to this neighborhood, are the following:

The Brotherhood Synagogue, 144 E. 20th Street, facing the park. A subtle Italianate building, with the aura of straitlaced Americana in its steep, curving wooden staircases and open, airy, simple prayer rooms on three floors. It was originally built for the Society of Friends in 1859.

Calvary Church on the corner of Park Avenue South and E. 21st Street. An exquisite Gothic Revival church with a gloomy, brooding exterior, it has bright stained-glass windows and an ornate interior that exudes warmth. Eleanor Roosevelt was baptized either in the church or the vicar's house. Theodore Roosevelt, who was born into a wealthy New York family at 28 E. 20th Street in 1858, was a parishioner here. Thomas Alva Edison is believed to have supervised the placement of an electric organ, one of the country's first, here. The Astor family, one of whose members went down with the Titanic, had a pew here. And when P. T. Barnum brought Jenny Lind to America, she sang here. Writer Edith Wharton may have prayed here occasionally; she lived nearby. Some guides think she was christened here; others think she may have been christened and definitely was married at the Serbian Orthodox Cathedral of St. Sava, at 15 W. 25th Street between Fifth and Sixth avenues, near Madison Square—her family's church. In those days it was Trinity, an Episcopal church. (Still another theory holds that Wharton was christened at Grace Church in the Village.)

Although its status rose in public estimation after it was declared a landmark, Gramercy Park remained an oasis of gentility—in part because the Third Avenue elevated train was torn down in the 1950s. New Yorkers, who prefer subways to buses for rapid transport, considered how long it would take them to get around town by bus from apartments in Gramercy Park, and many shunned the neighborhood for this reason. Though as quaint as Greenwich Village, with a rich, intriguing history, little Gramercy Park remains quieter, less bohemian, and less commercial—with fewer tourists and fewer walking tours.

To the southeast, some guides visit another bucolic park and enclave, around Stuyvesant Square. Here stands another historic church, St. George's, at 17th Street between Third and Second avenues. If a guide omits this square from the Gramercy Park tour, you might ask if a side trip is possible. Experienced guides such as Michael George are familiar with the architecture and social history of Stuyvesant Square. You will learn from Mr. George, for example, that the composer Antonín Dvořák lived in a neat little townhouse just off the square and wrote his "New World Symphony" there.

At the same time that Gramercy Park was developing, a neighborhood directly to the west across town, Chelsea, was springing up. Chelsea runs west of Sixth Avenue from Greenwich Village's northern border, 14th Street, to 23rd Street. Improved transportation, including horse-drawn vehicles and locomotives, began to make it feasible as well as attractive for people to live as far north as Chelsea—and even in the hinterlands of the Upper West Side—and still be able to get to the business section in downtown Manhattan with relative ease, aggravating traffic jams in muddy, unpaved streets notwithstanding. In Chelsea's heyday, in the first decades of the nineteenth century, a number of outstanding edifices were erected. The General Theological Seminary built beginning in 1825 and located between Ninth and Tenth avenues and 20th and 21st streets, was donated by Clement Clarke Moore, whose family had a farm in the neighborhood. The West Building, dating back to 1836, still stands. Moore also helped design the nearby English Gothic parish church, St. Peter's, on 20th Street between Eighth and Ninth avenues, built in 1836–38. A cemetery belonging to the Spanish and Portuguese Synagogue is located on 21st Street between Sixth and Seventh avenues, and a French church built in 1841, St. Vincent de Paul, stands on 23rd Street between Sixth and Seventh avenues. The Spanish Church of Our Lady of Guadalupe was built in 1860 on 14th Street between Seventh and Eighth avenues, on the stretch of 14th Street called "Little Spain." You can still see Spanish businesses here.

Far from being a church, Chelsea Place, 147 Eighth Avenue, between 17th and 18th streets, has reverberating music every night until 4:00 A.M. It's a popular nightclub, whose owner calls it a "speakeasy," in a landmark building. The official Chelsea Historic District runs from Ninth to Tenth avenues between 20th and 22nd streets. Chelsea, too, lost its cachet by the end of the nineteenth century, when its socially prominent residents in their fine houses, particularly in the West 20s, disdained the bohemian element moving into the neighborhood as roomers. Chelsea became a commercial area of small shopkeepers on the avenues, with apartment houses for working-class and middle-class residents on the side streets. The Chelsea Hotel on W. 23rd Street symbolizes the bohemian reputation that the neighborhood acquired; for decades the hotel has housed painters, sculptors, writers, musicians, and theater people, some of them eccentric, many world-famous.

Chelsea also started changing in the 1970s and '80s, as New Yorkers began to view the neighborhood as a prime location—convenient to all other neighborhoods and, for the most part, affordable to live in. Rents and cooperative apartment prices have climbed sharply in the last decade. Fashionable clubs and restaurants have opened, as they have in

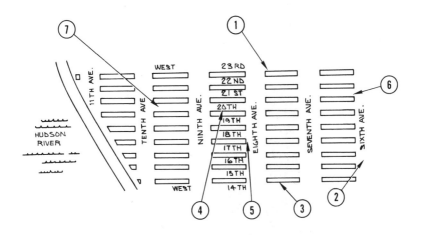

Points of Interest in Chelsea and the Left Side of Ladies' Mile

1. Chelsea Hotel
2. Sixth Avenue
3. "Little Spain"
4. St. Peter's Church

5. Chelsea Place
6. Spanish–Portuguese Jewish Cemetery
7. General Theological Seminary

Gramercy Park and the adjacent commercial neighborhood, the former Ladies' Mile.

Graceful Madison Square, at the northern end of Ladies' Mile, became especially notable by the 1880s, when architect Stanford White designed Madison Square Garden there. Other architecturally prominent commercial and public buildings stand in the vicinity, along with remaining brownstones of the Edith Wharton era. Not to be missed is the eerily antique visage of her family's church, called Trinity Chapel when she was married there in it the 1880s. Now it's the Serbian Orthodox Cathedral of St. Sava.

Just to the north of Madison Square and Gramercy Park, affluent New Yorkers developed another residential neighborhood. Elegant and quiet, a veritable twin-sister neighborhood to Gramercy Park, Murray Hill has never lost its luster. Deriving its appeal mainly from its elegantly tasteful architecture, it maintains the aura of a suburb. A hilly neighborhood, it was a perfect place for children to ride sleighs before World War I.

Marvin Gelfand's Walk of the Town tour begins at 23rd Street and Sixth Avenue for a view of Ladies' Mile from its northern end, then takes in the Chelsea Hotel, with its lobby paintings by residents and its colorful history. The tour moves southwest to the Episcopal General Theological Seminary; St. Peter's, a small Episcopalian church; and the row houses in the West Twenties, done in Greek Revival and Italianate styles. From the end of the Civil War until the 1880s—the gaslight era— this neighborhood reached its peak of social status. Old, socially prominent New York families lived in the row houses in the London Terrace area between W. 23rd and W. 24th streets and Ninth and Tenth avenues. In the 1890s, the character of Chelsea changed, becoming bohemian, with dilapidated rooming houses. In the western reaches, an Irish community developed. If Gelfand's tour groups are interested, he leads them to the Chelsea docks at the Hudson River at the tour's end.

Michael George, a teacher in New York University's School of Continuing Education, chooses Ladies' Mile and Chelsea as subjects for investigation. He scrutinizes the Ladies' Mile buildings, which were once emporiums, and the Chelsea brownstones, which were originally fashionable one-family houses and were later broken up into apartments. He recounts the history of Chelsea as a farm in the family of Clement Clarke Moore, who wrote the famous eighteenth-century poem "Twas the Night Before Christmas."

George pays particular attention to the Chelsea Hotel for its nineteenth-century architecture and continuing stream of important guests and residents in the arts—among them the late Irish playwright Brendan Behan and the author Clifford Irving, who stayed in the Chelsea during the controversy over his invented biography of billionaire Howard Hughes.

George also visits St. Peter's Episcopal Church and the landmark Episcopalian General Theological Seminary at Chelsea Square bordering Ninth and Tenth avenues and West 20th and 21st streets. From its pastoral campus, with its ivy-covered buildings, you can look southward for a view of the fine W. 20th Street row houses. Before the Seminary existed, ministers used to go to Scotland for ordination.

Val Ginter's Ginter-Gotham Urban History conducts a tour called "Shopping in the Nineteenth Century: A Mile of Victorian Fashion," from Gramercy Park to Madison Square, taking in more than sixty historic sights. Among them are the Calvary Episcopal Church and Sunday School Building on Park Avenue and 21st Street; many of the homes on Gramercy Park; and the statue of Edwin Booth as "Hamlet," which has stood in the park since 1918. On Third Avenue, just outside the historic Gramercy Park district, Tuesday's, built in 1894, a restaurant with a basement jazz club, Fat Tuesday's, is a stop on the tour. So is the very charming 19th Street between Irving Place and Third Avenue. With its Gothic Revival former coach houses and studios that were once popular residences for all types of artists, the block has been dubbed "The Block Beautiful." Theda Bara, the silent-screen star, was one of the well-known personalities who lived here.

On Irving Place, Ginter points out Pete's Tavern and the little red brick house in which Elizabeth Marbury and Elsie de Wolfe lived, from about 1890 to 1910. Ms. Marbury was well known as a theatrical and literary agent; Ms. de Wolfe, whose interior designs set fashion standards, went on stage and eventually married and settled in Europe as Lady Mendl.

Ginter talks about the Ladies' Mile stores dating back to Arnold Constable in 1869, moves to the Flatiron District (also known as the photo district), where he talks about the Flatiron Building, erected in 1902, the Barnes & Noble bookstore on Fifth Avenue and 19th Street, and the late-nineteenth-century buildings that served as headquarters for publisher Charles Scribner, the Sohmer Piano Company, and Western Union. At Madison Square and in the area directly north, he discusses the area's landmarks—historic buildings and statues—from the Serbian Orthodox Cathedral of St. Sava built as Trinity Chapel in 1855; to the awesome Metropolitan Life Insurance Company Building, with its ornate, decorative indoor mailboxes; to a Stanford White pied-à-terre, separate from his Gramercy Park home, which was built solely for parties; to the Gilsey House and the Grand Hotel—just two of the fine hotels that sprang up in the neighborhood beginning in 1871.

Ginter also does a 23d Street tour, walking from the East to the Hudson rivers, pointing out dozens of highlights, including Bellevue Hospital Center and the Veteran's Administration Medical Center, which can care for 15,000 patients a year; the isolated Waterside residential enclave, with its fine view of the river; and Asser Levy Place, named for the city's first kosher butcher, who arrived in Manhattan in 1654, when it was still New Amsterdam. Ginter also includes several historic churches and the fine art deco apartment house at 235 E. 22nd Street on his circuitous route—he takes many side trips. He stops at several sites on the fringes of Gramercy Park and Madison Square, and at the Flatiron Building, and then moves west to look at some former grand stores and the Chelsea Hotel, built in 1884. As all the tour leaders do, Ginter has some pet facts to impart that another tour leader might not have. He knows, for example, that the hotel's cast-iron balconies were made by the Cornell Iron Works and that among the celebrities who lived here were Mark Twain and Jane Fonda. Moving further west, he passes the C.B.S. Television studios where soap operas are taped; London Terrace's complex of fourteen buildings; the house at 450 W. 23rd Street where poet Edwin Arlington Robinson lived; the Empire Diner, which dates back to 1943 and now attracts a trendy clientele; and the site of a historic restaurant, Cavanaugh's, which attracted Diamond Jim Brady and Lillian Russell.

Joyce Gold counts Chelsea as one of her specialties, to which she takes groups for two-hour walks by appointment. Her lecture also recounts the beginnings of the neighborhood as the farm of eighteenth-century poet Clement Clarke Moore. The farm, which had been in Moore's family for at least two generations, was broken up when it came into conflict with the city's grid system.

Ms. Gold also talks about the pretty little neighborhood between Ninth and Tenth avenues in the West 20s, with its row houses. In the nineteenth century, the neighborhood served as a theater district and housed Tin Pan Alley and several great department stores.

Moving on to nearby Ladies' Mile, Ms. Gold concentrates on a thirty-year period encompassing the gaslight era and the Gay Nineties, when shopping in massive department stores became a form of recreation for women. Because of their enduring utilitarianism, these buildings, many of which are interesting from an architectural point of view, may one day qualify for landmark designation. Some community groups are lobbying for it, and they may be helped in their efforts by the many prestigious publishing houses and other companies that are moving their offices from extremely expensive, modern Upper East Side spaces into this older neighborhood.

Bill Harris, a writer and former partner in the tour firm Viewpoint International, chooses Gramercy Park as one of his favorite tour destinations. He treats it as an art tour and discusses the artists, writers, actors, and publishers who lived either on or near the park—Edith Wharton, O. Henry, Mark Twain, and Edwin Booth, who helped to found the Players Club, among them. Harris also discusses the obvious beauty of the square and its conception and development.

Harris's other favorite tour spot is Murray Hill, which he describes as a charming, quiet neighborhood in which to live. He discusses the elegant nineteenth-century architecture, in particular the landmark Sniffen Court, at 150–158 E. 36th Street, between Third and Lexington avenues, built in 1850–60—a quiet mews with ten Romanesque Revival brick carriage houses.

Harris also brings up legend and lore. For instance, baseball was supposedly played during the Civil War era and perhaps earlier, at Lexington and 34th Street and also to the west, at Madison Square, by neighborhood men looking for recreation and exercise on weekends. And even if Abner Doubleday did invent baseball in Cooperstown, New York, where the Baseball Hall of Fame stands, a plaque on the corner of 34th Street and Lexington Avenue says that baseball was invented on that spot.

Murray Hill's name came from a Revolutionary War partisan, Robert Murray, whose wife helped detain the British in this hilly neighborhood while General George Washington marched safely across Manhattan.

Barry Lewis loves to tour Ladies' Mile, which was built up in the post-Civil War era and served as midtown Manhattan until the turn of the century. He begins his walk at Tenth Street and Broadway, near Grace (Episcopal) Church, 800 Broadway, a fine Gothic Revival church, designed by James Renwick, Jr., a structural engineer and architect, in 1846, and walks up Broadway to Union Square at 14th Street. The park has been renovated; and luxury housing has replaced the old, abandoned department store, Klein's on the Square, a bargain-hunter's paradise until it closed in the early 1970s. And from the square's vantage point, where a farmer's market functions full-blast on Wednesdays, Fridays, and Saturdays selling vegetables, fruits, plants, and homemade cakes, cookies, jellies, and even smoked game, Lewis points out the fine vista of Broadway above the square.

Sooty though the old department stores on Broadway may look, they tantalize architecture buffs. A handsome, ornate, cast-iron, Second Empire-style building at the corner of Broadway and 20th Street housed Lord and Taylor from 1869 to 1914. (Lord and Taylor had a store on

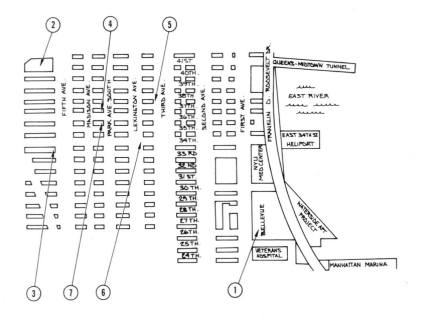

Points of Interest in Murray Hill

1. Bellevue Hospital
2. New York Public Library main building
3. Empire State Building
4. Morgan Library
5. Sniffen Court
6. Baseball plaque
7. Church of the Incarnation

Grand Street in Lower Manhattan in the 1850s before that and eventually moved to its current Fifth Avenue and 38th Street site.)

Ever wonder what happened to Adams Dry Goods? Or Siegel-Cooper? Never even heard of them? Siegel-Cooper was a popular Ladies' Mile clothing store, which closed in 1914. Lewis makes it come alive again in his lecture.

Arthur Marks has invented the "Age of Innocence" tour, borrowing the title from Edith Wharton's classic novel. He leads it for various groups, including The New-York Historical Society and the Lambda Legal Defense and Education Fund, Inc. He begins at Gilsey House, 1200 Broadway at 29th Street, a striking cast-iron building with a mansard roof and a diagonal tower topped by a clock. Clocks were placed outside buildings for the public's convenience in the late nineteenth century. Ladies never wore watches in those days, and men found it too much trouble to take out their timepieces—especially in cold weather and in the dark.

From there the tour moves to the Appellate Division of the New York State Supreme Court, at 27 Madison Avenue, an exuberantly decorated English manor made of marble. The court building, noted for its murals and statuary inside and outside, was paid for with $600,000 of federal money, one-third of which went into the decorations. The tour then visits Cass Gilbert's New York Life Building, on the northern corner of Madison Square, then walks down to Gramercy Park to the National Arts Club. After a brief discussion of its social and architectural history— two townhouses were joined to make a private residence for Governor Samuel J. Tilden of New York more than 100 years ago—the tour group usually enters the club for a reception. (Tilden was the Presidential candidate who won the popular vote and lost the election in the electoral college.)

Marks also leads a tour in Murray Hill by special appointment, beginning at the Church of the Incarnation at E. 35th Street and Madison Avenue (whose minister married Franklin and Eleanor Roosevelt). The tour passes by Sniffen Court, the Empire State Building, B. Altman's department stores, and the centrally air-conditioned Church of Our Saviour at 38th Street and Park Avenue. Marks is enthusiastic about Murray Hill, describing it as an attractively preserved neighborhood close to the center of everything happening in town.

Richard McDermott leads tours of Ladies' Mile and Gramercy Park as two of his specialties.

His Ladies' Mile tour begins at Broadway and 10th Street, where he discusses Grace Church and the fashionable houses, hotels, and stores in the area. He tells you about A. T. Stewart, who had a department store south of Grace Church; Stewart was one of the pioneers of department stores. The building known as The New York Sun Building, in which he had his first emporium—possibly the first department store in the country—still stands in Lower Manhattan near City Hall.

McDermott moves up to Union Square Park, mentioning the efforts of community groups to have Ladies' Mile, including some buildings on the fringes of Union Square Park, designated landmarks. One Union Square West building originally housed Tiffany's. And Tiffany's, McDermott tells you, bought twenty miles of Atlantic Cable, after one of the first attempts to lay it failed in the nineteenth century. The store stripped it and made jewelry and artifacts from the copper, marking the items as certifiable Atlantic Cable. According to McDermott, Tiffany's still has some copper from the cable left. The story may be apocryphal, but it's charming to hear McDermott tell it nonetheless.

He also claims that many of the Paris labels on clothes sold on Ladies' Mile were forgeries; and that Singer Sewing Machines, which were sold on Ladies' Mile—and were an improvement on existing sewing machines—were invented by Isaac Singer (no relationship to the Nobel Prize-winning writer Isaac Bashevis Singer), in partnership with a member of an old New York family. After Singer died at a relatively young age, his estate became entangled in litigation. He had managed to marry five wives and have twenty-five children, juggling his families by telling them that he had to travel for business a great deal, says McDermott. When they found out the truth, they sued—not such a strange occurrence, when you realize that as you sew, so shall you reap.

McDermott discusses the idosyncrasies of one owner of a Union Square house which has neither been rented, sold, or used in years. Then he moves up Broadway, discussing the foibles and excesses of some of the well-known women who once shopped here. The area bounded by Broadway and Sixth Avenue and 14th and 23rd streets was home to Macy's, Lord and Taylor, Arnold Constable, Siegel-Cooper, B. Altman's, Hugh O'Neill's, and Adams Dry Goods, as well as several other great stores whose names passed from the scene long ago. The area boasts a large ensemble of nineteenth-century commercial architecture—"which needs to be scrubbed, not bulldozed," says McDermott, echoing the sentiments of many guides and neighborhood buffs.

From there, McDermott moves up to Gramercy Park, where he talks about the neighborhood's varied architectural styles and recounts some ribald tales about past residents. For example, actor John Garfield was found dead in a young woman's apartment in a building at 3 Gramercy Park West. A policeman who claims he was called to the scene on the night of the death has told McDermott that Garfield was found being placed in a hallway. And a block away from the park, in a house facing the Gramercy Park Hotel, a wealthy spinster, granddaughter of Peter Cooper, founder of Cooper Union, died and left a bizarre legacy of a large collection of pornography. McDermott also visits the interiors of Calvary Church and the National Arts Club, and he discusses the membership of the Players Club next door. When James Cagney lived on the park, for instance, he used to have lunch in the club very often with equally famous friends. The clubs are open to the public and nonmembers by appointment and invitation only.

McDermott gives his Ladies' Mile and Gramercy Park tours several times a year for the Union Square Park Community Coalition, which is lobbying to achieve landmark status for Ladies' Mile.

The **Municipal Art Society,** in line with its policy of sponsoring a variety of tours that tend to change from year to year, presented a tour called "Parks, People and Monuments" in 1988. Marvin Gelfand led people to Union Square Park, Gramercy Park, and Madison Square to see the memorials erected to public heroes, with a discussion of the social, political, and artistic inspirations for the sculpture and for vest-pocket parks in general.

The **Museum of the City of New York** tours "Ladies' Mile: the Gilded Age Retail and Entertainment Center," as Hope Cooke, the museum's tour coordinator, has called it. She walks from Union Square to Madison Square, viewing the buildings that once housed fashionable hotels, popular theaters, palatial department stores, and restaurants frequented by Diamond Jim Brady and actress Lillian Russell. (One of Brady's favorite places was Luchow's, an atmospheric German restaurant, east of Union Square, dating back to the early nineteenth century. It remained a leading light of the neighborhood until it closed recently.) Cooke presents the intriguing thesis that the neighborhood's flowering in the nineteenth century set the stage for the American ethic of conspicuous consumption. It was here that shopping became a recreational pastime that was soon adopted by the entire country.

The New-York Historical Society tours Gramercy Park, beginning at the New York Life Insurance Company Building, at 27th Street and Madison Avenue, passing the Appellate Division of the Supreme Court of New York, and continuing down to Madison Square Park. The tour also visits the Serbian Cathedral of St. Sava, where novelist Edith Wharton was married, when it was Trinity Chapel in 1885, then walks to the E. 20th Street mansion near Gramercy Park on the site of which President Theodore Roosevelt was born, then to the Gramercy Park Hotel at the corner of 21st Street and Lexington Avenue, where Stanford White's house once stood. The group walks around the park to the National Arts Club, a very pretty private club with Moorish arches in its interior, for a reception that ends the tour.

The **92nd Street "Y"** sponsors a tour, "Midtown South," led by Joyce Mendelsohn, to Madison Square, where Stanford White was assassinated in the roof-garden restaurant of his own Madison Square Garden. Harry K. Thaw, the deranged and jealous husband of a beautiful actress, Evelyn Nesbitt, possibly White's mistress, certainly one of his many girlfriends, shot White. Though that Garden is gone, other buildings extant in the neighborhood make intriguing lecture fodder. Ms. Mendlelsohn heads to Gramercy Park and visits the Players and National Arts clubs as well as the mansion on the site of which President Theodore Roosevelt was born; she ends the tour at Union Square Park, with a talk about Ladies' Mile and the current rejuvenation of the neighborhood.

Another "Y" tour visits the Chelsea Hotel at 222 W. 23rd St., between Seventh and Eighth avenues, a Victorian Gothic building dating back to 1884, with delicate iron balconies and a long history as a refuge for artists, writers, and composers. Among its residents have been writer Thomas Wolfe (*You Can't Go Home Again*); poets Dylan Thomas (*Under Milkwood*) and Edgar Lee Masters (*The Spoon River Anthology*); musician Virgil Thompson, who still lives there, and painter Jackson Pollock, the abstract expressionist. The hotel is a repository of everything from touching human stories to the lurid murder of British punk star Sid Vicious's girlfriend. But most of all it's a place for artists to be themselves. One of the hotel residents, Meryl Lister, a dancer and choreographer, led the 1988 tour, introducing tourists to some other well-known artistic souls in residence there—Thompson for one.

Arthur Marks leads a "Y"-sponsored tour of designers, decorators, photographers, and even a caterer's business in the general vicinity of Ladies' Mile. Everything has become so trendy in New York, Marks notes, that nobody could resist nicknaming the area of his tour: Sofi (an acronym for *S*outh *o*f the *F*latiron Building). Sofi runs roughly from 14th Street and Fifth Avenue to the convergence of Broadway and Fifth Avenue at 23rd Street, the site of the Flatiron Building, near Madison Park.

On one occasion, Marks began this tour at a caterer's luxurious working-living loft at 73 Fifth Avenue. Called Table of Contents, the firm displays newspaper clippings about the parties it has catered. Naturally, the clients have been wealthy and fashionable people and organizations. As Marks expounded upon the coming-of-age of Sofi as a district filled with photographers and other artistic people involved in the exciting visual decorations in town, Table of Contents chefs cooked and served hors d'oeuvres: coconut-flake-studded cheese balls with fresh raspberry centers; walnuts on cheese encasing grapes; chicken medallions stuffed with wild mushrooms and dabs of mustard sauce. Oh, this is living! If you can afford it, you become a customer. If not, for a small tour fee, you could have a taste of a dream world that constitutes real life in elegant circles. Then you toured the living area of Table of Contents' owner before you set out for various other trendy businesses, walking west toward Chelsea, in the side streets off Fifth Avenue.

Note: The "Y" doesn't necessarily schedule exactly the same tours every year. But the Gramercy Park-Ladies' Mile-Chelsea neighborhoods are a regular, annual destination. Check with the "Y" for each year's changing itineraries and tour leaders.

New York Walkabout calls its Stuyvesant Square/Gramercy Park tour the "Islands of Gentility" walk. It starts at 14th Street and Third Avenue, from which it is a short walk to quiet, peaceful Gramercy Park, which runs from 20th to 21st streets, between Third and Park avenues. It's also approachable at Lexington Avenue at 21st St. and at Irving Place, which runs from 14th to 20th streets.

New York Walkabout also has a "Tin Pan Alley/Madison Square" tour about the days when the neighborhood was a leading entertainment district, with theaters, Tin Pan Alley, and the first two Madison Square Gardens.

The firm's Murray Hill tour is titled "Remnants of a Gilded Age." Some of the highlights are Sniffen Court, the Delamar Mansion, the former J. P. Morgan Jr. house, and the Pierpont Morgan Library, at 33 E. 36th Street, between Madison and Park avenues. McKim, Mead and White, the prominent architectural firm, built the elegant library in 1906. Morgan used it to house his collection of rare books and manuscripts.

Pete Salwen's Mark Twain tour reaches Gramercy Park to visit the Players Club, which Twain helped found. See Salwen's tour outlined in chapter 3.

John Tauranac, an architectural historian, views Gramercy Park as a gem and concentrates on the history of the park, the development of the neighborhood, and its architecture. He focuses on such people as James Harper of the Harper and Row publishing firm, who had a house on the west side of the park, and the unusual "Mayors lamps" that grace the entrance. Harper was also a New York City mayor and banned livestock from the streets in the nineteenth century. The National Arts Club and the Players Club, of course, figure in the lecture and itinerary.

Tauranac's Murray Hill tour begins at the Empire State Building and B. Altman's department store, on the corner of 35th Street and Fifth Avenue. He heads east into Murray Hill for an examination of the variety of architectural styles found in the area's turn-of-the-century row houses. Tauranac's fancy is especially taken with the blocks bounded by Park and Lexington avenues and 35th and 36th streets and with the Delamar Mansion and the Morgan Library. The tour heads uptown to 42nd Street and Fifth Avenue, ending in front of the lions of a great classical Beaux Arts building, the New York Public Library.

Gerard Wolfe, a guide with a scholarly orientation, has written extensively about the walking-tour life. His recently reissued *New York: A Guide to the Metropolis, Walking Tours of Architecture and History* (New York: McGraw-Hill, 1988) constitutes an easy-to-read armchair as well as practical guide to many of the city's important historic buildings. For those who would rather read than walk, the book is entertaining, buttressed by tantalizing tidbits of social history. In his book and for his walking tours, he pays substantial attention to Ladies' Mile and is particularly authoritative about the stores in the district and the transportation network in town during the Ladies' Mile era. He begins with the site of Wanamaker Department Store, at 770 Broadway. The cast-iron building was destroyed in a fire in 1956, and then a condominium called Stewart House was built there at 8th Street in Greenwich Village. Wolfe progresses up Broadway past Grace Church and the 11th-Street building that once hosted Presidents Lincoln and Grant, Buffalo Bill Cody, Sarah Bernhardt, and P. T. Barnum, when it was the Hotel St. Denis. As several guides do, Wolfe mentions that Alexander Graham Bell demonstrated his telephone to a startled audience here. Wolfe talks about the nearby James J. McCreery Store, started by an enterprising immigrant who also became an influential art patron. Toward the end of the century he moved his store from Broadway and 11th Street to Sixth Avenue and 23rd Street, on Ladies' Mile; the Broadway building still survives. Wolfe covers Rogers Peet Company, Wallack's Theater, and finally reaches Union Square, where he discusses some of the famous stores that once stood there, including R. H. Macy's at 56 W. 14th Street; you can still see the store's faded sign, which was emblazoned on a stone panel.

Wolfe cuts across 14th Street to Sixth Avenue, where he points out the cast-iron building that once housed B. Altman & Company. All the while he discusses the careers of the great merchants of the neighborhood. Siegel-Cooper & Company is included; so are Simpson Crawford & Simpson, Cammeyer's, Hugh O'Neill's, Adams Dry Goods, Ehrich Brothers, Riker's Drug Company (later absorbed into the Liggett chain), Best & Company, Bonwit Teller, LeBoutillier, Flint & Horner Furniture Company, Stern Brothers Department Store, and a store called "The Linen Store," James McCutcheon & Company. Wending his way back toward Broadway, he talks about the Sohmer Piano Company, Charles Scribner's Sons' first building, which still has an *S* on the fourth-floor balcony, and a colony of publishers of books on religion. At Broadway, he takes you to the southwest corner of 20th Street and shows you the ornate, iron-front building that once housed Lord and Taylor, a family enterprise, Arnold Constable, which began on Pine Street and survived for 150 years, and W. J. Sloane, at one time carpet and rug headquarters for the country, started by a young Scotch weaver. Along the way, too, Wolfe notes some of the churches and other historic, noncommercial sights.

His Gramercy Park tour pays particular attention to some of the best-known historic and architectural sites, taking into account "the Block Beautiful"—the charming collection of old townhouses on 19th Street between Irving Place and Third Avenue—and continues down to 14th Street for a view of the Con Edison Energy Museum and a discussion of the old Academy of Music, a cavernous building dating back to 1854 that was replaced by Con Ed; and also the late lamented Luchow's.

Wolfe's Madison Square tour provides a detailed look at the history of the social and entertainment scene in this neighborhood, including the turn-of-the-century headquarters of Time-Life Magazine, Madison Square Park itself, and historic, religious and commercial buildings, including the Toy Center Building on the corner of 23rd Street and Broadway, facing Madison Square Park. The toy center stands on the site of what was once the city's most luxurious hotel, the Fifth Avenue—a favorite gathering place for the city's wheelers and dealers from the 1850s to the turn of the century.

In Chelsea, Wolfe visits the historic district and also many of the sights with particular cachet or lore, among them the Grand Opera House, which stood on the northwest corner of Eighth Avenue and 23rd Street. It was owned by financiers Jay Gould and Jim Fisk; Fisk's mistress was a star in the theater, and she also became romantically involved with a former partner of Fisk's, Edward S. Stokes. Their quarrels and resultant lawsuits showed up in the newspapers and eventually ended when Stokes shot Fisk to death. The winner was Jay Gould, who continued to operate the theater.

For architecture buffs, the Wolfe tour of Chelsea's historic district is very edifying, too.

Chapter Seven

East and West
Midtown Manhattan

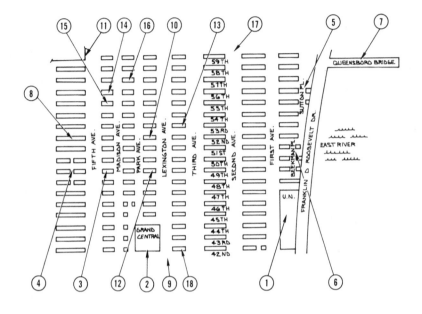

Points of Interest in Midtown, East Side

1. United Nations Headquarters
2. Grand Central Terminal
3. St. Patrick's Cathedral
4. Rockefeller Center
5. Sutton Place
6. Beekman Place
7. Queensboro Bridge
8. Museum of Modern Art
9. Chanin Building
10. Seagram's Building
11. Central Park South
12. Waldorf Astoria
13. St. Peter's Lutheran Church
14. IBM
15. AT&T
16. Fuller Building
17. Tramway to Roosevelt Island
18. Chrysler Building

It's so busy and raucous and, in places, so exquisitely pretty and elegant that midtown Manhattan seems obvious and easy for anyone to find, from the famed Times Square billboards and the 1 Times Square Building to the landmark Grand Central Terminal. But the fine points and the history of these world-renowned places are sure to escape the hurried or casual visitor, who has no guide to prompt appreciation and comprehension.

By the turn of the century, the theater district had made its final change of venue, moving up from Madison Square to Times Square, near the convergence of Broadway and Seventh Avenue with W. 42nd Street. Many of the theaters from that era are still standing, having recently acquired landmark status. The oldest one operating as a legitimate theater is the Lyceum, a neo-Rennaissance building with a fluted canopy over the entrance, built in 1903.

Grand Central Terminal symbolizes the transportation revolution in this country that began in 1871. That's when Commodore Cornelius Vanderbilt put up a huge depot with a cast-iron and glass train shed on the site of the present Grand Central Terminal; the current Beaux Arts building was erected in 1913. But Vanderbilt's original Grand Central depot signaled the expansion of transportation in the Northeast and the growing influence of New York on the nation's economy.

Also in midtown, one finds scores of art deco masterpieces, among them the Chrysler Building on E. 42nd Street and Radio City Music Hall in the original Rockefeller Center complex, which runs from Fifth to Sixth avenues and from 48th to 51st streets. One of the country's most important museums, the Museum of Modern Art, built by the Rockefellers, on W. 53rd Street between Fifth and Sixth avenues, stands in this busy neighborhood. And at the gateway to the Upper West Side, the Rockefeller-assisted Lincoln Center for the Performing Arts, a magisterial sight, especially with its buildings alight at night, symbolizes the quintessence of New York's contemporary glamor. Philip Johnson and Eero Saarinen were among the many architects involved in the Lincoln Center design. Many other leading architects of the twentieth century have contributed to the face of midtown Manhattan.

Some guides and institutions sponsor tours to midtown for the history and architecture and for preservationist activities. Several buildings run their own guided tours, including Radio City Music Hall, the Seagram Building on Park Avenue at 53rd Street, and Lincoln Center for the Performing Arts. The Metropolitan Opera Guild sponsors an intriguing tour of the Met's backstage, within Lincoln Center's complex. The *New York Times* occasionally permits public tours. And the National Broadcasting Company (NBC) has many tours daily to its newsrooms and studios.

The **Art Deco Society**'s tours provide a feast for the eyes in this neighborhood. Tours visit, for example, the Chanin and Chrysler buildings, Rockefeller Center, the Empire State Building—all landmarks built in the 1920s and 1930s—and scores of other structures. The 1929 Chanin Building stands at 122 E. 42nd Street at Lexington Avenue, and features floral decorations in terra-cotta at the base and mock Gothic buttresses above the fourth floor. The Chrysler Building, at 405 Lexington Avenue between E. 42nd and E. 43rd streets, was designed by architect William Van Alen in 1930. The building features a Nirosta metal spire of sparkling arches rising to a point—a striking sight in the city's skyline. As a reminder that the building belonged to an automobile manufacturer, gargoyles shaped like radiator caps of vintage cars decorate the setbacks. Brick designs modeled after automobile tires adorn the walls. The Empire State Building, 350 Fifth Avenue at W. 34th Street, built in 1931, reigned for a long time as the world's tallest building. It was originally supposed to have 86 stories. Then the builders decided it needed the finishing touch of a mooring mast for dirigibles. Though the mast was never operational, it brought the building to a height of 102 stories and 1,250 feet. The building immediately became a tourist attraction. During the Depression era, the fees paid by tourists going to the observation deck paid the building's taxes. The vital statistics on this building—73 elevators, 7 miles of elevator shafts, 6,500 windows, 60 miles of water pipes—are staggering. The building is open daily from 9:30 A.M. to midnight.

Rockefeller Center was designed by a committee of architects throughout the 1930s. It is recognized as the city's greatest urban complex, sheathed in gray Indiana limestone, with the Channel Gardens leading from Fifth Avenue to a sunken plaza. Paul Manship's dazzling golden statue of Prometheus stealing fire from the gods presides over the plaza. It contains an outdoor restaurant in summer, which in winter is transformed into a popular ice-skating rink, where excellent performers give free shows, all winter.

Art Tours of Manhattan takes groups by special arrangement to notable midtown museums and art collections, such as the Museum of Modern Art and the Museum of American Folk Art.

Backstage on Broadway presents a 10:30 A.M. tour Monday through Saturday, beginning with a lecture on how a Broadway show is put together, in whatever theater is available for the day. Actors, stage managers, and other theater personnel describe how a show progresses from its conception to opening night and even road shows.

Often the Edison Theatre on W. 47th Street between Broadway and Eighth Avenue serves as the tour's workshop. You must call the office to be sure and reserve a place.

East and West Midtown Manhattan

Friends of Central Park leads all types of walking and bus tours throughout the year in Manhattan, New Jersey, and sometimes even upstate New York and foreign countries. However, since the required $1 donations for some of its overnight, annual extravaganza walks through Harlem, through the Hudson tubes to New Jersey, or across the Brooklyn Bridge go to benefit the trees—about 24,000 at last count—in Central Park, we'll note this group's tours in the section on Midtown Manhattan. Not a tour leader, except on special occasions—e.g., an American Institute of Architects convention—but with a related mission, the group called the Central Park Conservancy has been reclaiming the park from graffiti and vandalism, planting trees, flowers and shrubs, and inviting volunteers and interns to help in the effort. Call 360–8236 for information about the Conservancy.

Marvin Gelfand's Walk of the Town sponsors a theater-district tour as one of its specialties. Gelfand visits the old theaters still standing and the sites of long-gone, historic theaters, talking about legendary performers and plays. Broadway has fewer theaters now than it had at the turn of the century, but its mystique endures. About eighty years ago, a critic looked down one of the side streets in the West Forties from Times Square and marveled at the brightness of the lights and the marquees, which symbolized the brilliant culture of the district. He would have the same view today.

Michael George, the official tour leader for Classical America, leads walks to various parts of midtown for that group and for the Municipal Art Society, on whose Board of Directors he has served. He also takes his classes from the N.Y.U. School of Continuing Education on forays to scrutinize midtown's variety. His M.A.S. tours are issue-oriented—focusing, for example, on quality of life, zoning, the livableness of the city, or the future of Columbus Circle. On M.A.S. tours, landmark issues are important. For example, these days, the M.A.S. is raising the question of how shady Central Park should be, because of proposed construction that would cast a large shadow over the park.

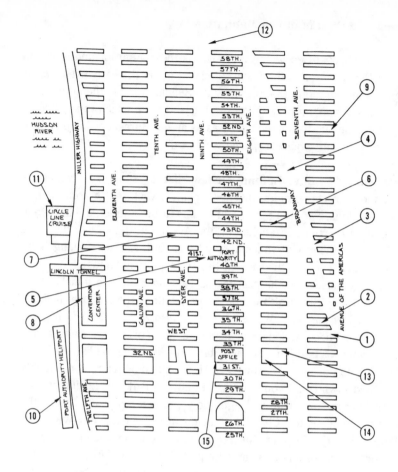

Points of Interest in Midtown, West Side

1. Herald Square
2. Macy's Herald Square
3. Times Square/theater district
4. TKTS Broadway tickets half-price booth
5. Port Authority Bus Terminal
6. *New York Times*
7. Mitchell Lama Housing for musicians and entertainers
8. Jacob Javits Convention Center
9. W.C. Handy Place
10. Port Authority Heliport
11. Circle Line Cruise
12. Columbus Circle and the Coliseum area
13. Madison Square Garden
14. Pennsylvania Station
15. Main Post Office

East and West Midtown Manhattan

For Michael George, every walk has the goal of looking at a New York City vista for its own sake. At class time in the early evenings, he may take a group to the Empire State Building, or, via the 60th Street-Second Avenue tramway, to Roosevelt Island, from which vantage point, overlooking Manhattan, he discusses its architecture, allowing people to stand back and acquire a special view of the city.

Val Ginter's Ginter-Gotham Urban History sponsors a variety of tours in all parts of midtown. They include a walk past historic theater sites, beginning at 39th Street and ending at 59th Street; a 42nd Street tour from the United Nations on First Avenue in the east to the Hell's Kitchen neighborhood—once a very tough and wild area—along Ninth and Tenth avenues in the west Forties and Fifties; and a 57th Street tour from Sutton Place in the east to the Passenger Ship Terminal on the Hudson River. Ginter also offers a survey tour of the midtown building boom, which he calls "Will They Ever Finish Midtown?" And he, too, leads an art deco walking tour in several parts of town, including midtown, with visits to the Empire State Building; the Madison-Belmont Building on the southeast corner of Madison and 34th Street; the highly regarded Town House, on 38th Street between Park and Lexington avenues, built in 1930, with its bright, polychromed terra-cotta crown; the Chanin Building; the Chrysler Building at 405 Lexington Avenue at 42nd Street; the Graybar Building at 420 Lexington Avenue, which is the art deco portion of Grand Central's "Terminal City" and which houses some famous national magazine headquarters; the luxurious Waldorf Astoria Hotel; *Newsweek*'s building at 444 Madison Avenue; and Rockefeller Center, to name a few of his choices.

Ginter also does a jazz tour of town, ranging from Harlem to Greenwich Village. Usually he conducts this tour by bus, but at each part of town with historic jazz sights, he takes people for a stroll. In midtown, the great attraction is 52nd Street, with W. C. Handy Place between Sixth and Seventh avenues and Swing Street officially running between Fifth and Sixth avenues right past the Columbia Broadcasting System's front door. Imbedded in the sidewalk are plaques which pay tribute to some of the great musicians who played in clubs on this street:

trumpeter Roy Eldridge, pianist Art Tatum, violinist Stuff Smith, tenor saxophonist Lester Young, singer Billie Holliday, alto saxophonist Charlie Parker, trumpeter Dizzy Gillespie, tenor saxophonist Coleman Hawkins, drummer Kenny Clarke, singer Sarah Vaughan, pianist Thelonius Monk, and trumpeter Miles Davis.

During his tour of the theater district, Ginter points out such intriguing details as the site of the former Broadway Theatre, where Edwin Booth gave his last performance; the New Amsterdam Theatre on W. 42nd Street, built by producers Klaw and Erlanger in 1903, with a roof garden that was remodeled in 1915 to accommodate Flo Ziegfeld; the Times Square Theatre at 219 W. 42nd Street, where Gertrude Lawrence and Noël Coward performed in his play *Private Lives* in 1930; and many other theaters where historic performances by Lynn Fontanne, George M. Cohan, John Barrymore, Sr., and Tyrone Power took place. Ginter shows the building on the west side of Broadway between 43rd and 44th streets where the Paramount Theatre lured kids to cut afternoon classes for decades beginning in 1926; and Town Hall, at 113 W. 43rd Street, designed in 1921 by McKim, Mead & White and still presenting some of the best musical events in town. Ginter has sometimes ended his tour at the Columbus Circle subway kiosk, built on the site of Hearst's International Theatre, which spent its last years as home to N.B.C.'s "Your Show of Shows" with Sid Caesar and Imogene Coca.

On his Times Square tour, Ginter talks about the heyday early in the century of chic "lobster palaces," restaurants for theatergoers. Then the area became "the epicenter of low life," as he describes the social decline in the mid-twentieth century. But Times Square is currently being renovated in parts and is clearly on the upswing. Ginter brings along old photos of interiors of the theaters, many of them long gone, to illustrate his historic points.

Ginter's tour of "boomtown" midtown includes the General Motors Building and Trump Tower, both on Fifth Avenue; the AT&T Building at 550 Madison Avenue; the Citicorp Building, including St. Peter's Lutheran Church, which prompted a building boom on Third Avenue beginning in the late 1970s; and the tube skyscraper at 780 Third Avenue, which now houses *Newsday*'s Manhattan offices on a high floor with a panoramic view. There's no resemblance at all to the romantic old image of a ramshackle, homey newspaper office.

At the eastern end of 57th Street, Ginter begins at the Queensboro Bridge, stops at provincial-looking townhouses on Sutton Place, and walks west for views of some of the best postmodern architecture in town. He stops at the Fuller Building at 45 E. 57th Street, built in 1929 and a fine example of art deco architecture, points out 724 Fifth Avenue, which now houses some of the city's most prestigious art galleries, and continues past the Russian Tea Room, Carnegie Hall, which dates back to 1891, the 1909 Alwyn Court, which has undergone extensive refurbishing to give it a skylit atrium; the CBS Broadcast Center at 518 W. 57th Street, and ends at the N.Y.C. Passenger Ship Terminal, Port Authority of New York and New Jersey, which used to be a berth for the superliners. The *QE II* still berths there today. This tour is for elegance, not ethnicity.

Ginter also leads a midtown tour called "Women in the Architectonic Process." He notes that while many women have worked for architectural firms that designed important midtown buildings, the firms' names, not those of the women, have survived as the architects. Ginter highlights the role women artists and architects have played in designing New York's cityscape. He begins the tour in front of the Philip Morris Building, which was designed by Francoise Bollack of the firm of Ulrich Franzen. Ginter points out the former Union Carbide Building on Park Avenue, which was designed by Natalie DeBlois, and the Paine Webber Building at the Equitable Center on Sixth Avenue at 52nd Street, designed by Pat Swan of Skidmore, Owings and Merrill. In Ginter's view, one of the finest contributions by a woman is the three circular plaques on the exterior of Radio City Music Hall—Drama, Song, and Dance—by Hildreth Meiers.

He also talks about the roles played by Joy Buba and Carolyn Hood in the design of Rockefeller Center and sculptress Louise Nevelson's contribution to St. Peter's Lutheran Church at the Citicorp Building.

Grand Central Terminal has a free tour every Wednesday at 12:30 P.M. Quite frequently, Val Ginter, who designed the tour in partnership with Michael George, leads the tour; occasionally, other guides do the job. George and Ginter designed the tour in the mid-1970s as part of a campaign to save the terminal from further demolition. The tour was initially sponsored by the Municipal Art Society; now there is corporate funding, too. Every Wednesday, the guide hired by the M.A.S. meets the visitors' group under the Kodak sign in the main concourse of the terminal for a ninety-minute walk.

Guides point out myriad details: from the terminal's newly restored skylights, which had been blacked out during World War II as a precaution taken during air-raid drills, to the concourse ceiling, which is a foot higher than the nave of the cavernous Cathedral Church of St. John the Divine on Morningside Heights. Groups explore this magnificent Beaux Arts building from top to bottom, going outside to view the statuary facing 42nd Street, then finding a vantage point to view the underground loops of tracks. The buildings around the terminal have no basements, because of the network of tracks under the street. Eventually the group winds up on the fifth-floor glass catwalk, which is about one inch thick and slightly buoyant underfoot. Located high above the main concourse, the catwalk is almost close enough to enable a visitor to touch the stars in the constellations depicted on the ceiling.

By the end of the tour, visitors have learned about the history of transportation in the Northeast as well as the legendary public building and its sphere of influence.

Lincoln Center for the Performing Arts offers six to eight tours seven days a week between 10:00 A.M. and 5:00 P.M. The guides talk about the history of the buildings—what was imported and donated to create the Metropolitan Opera House, the New York State Theater, Avery Fisher Hall, the auditoriums of all the buildings, the Promenade, and the artworks. The lecture includes the library, which is open to the public without a tour, and also discusses (but does not visit) the Vivian Beaumont Theatre and Alice Tully Hall. Visitors can see Damrosch Park, the outdoor bandshell, on their own. Call 685-1800 to confirm the daily schedule.

East and West Midtown Manhattan

Arthur Marks, by appointment, leads an art deco tour of midtown, including the Chanin and Chrysler buildings on E. 42nd Street, Radio City Music Hall, and the Empire State Building. For extensive art deco tours in the midtown area, Mr. Marks suggests that a group hire a bus and walk around at various far-flung sites.

The **Metropolitan Opera House** has its own tour, sponsored by the Metropolitan Opera Guild, whose offices are located in a building facing Lincoln Center Plaza. The 1½-hour tour takes place Mondays through Fridays at 3:45 P.M. and on Saturdays at 10:30 A.M. You may meet the tour group in the Met's lobby, but you must reserve a place in advance. You will be escorted through the extensive wardrobe department and see scores of props, some of which are being repaired. You will pass rehearsal rooms and will sometimes overhear the Met's singers in preparatory work.

The **Municipal Art Society** has recently sponsored tours of W. 57th Street, which is being changed from a neighborhood of low-rent buildings and shops to a towering urban center, with developments planned for Roosevelt Hospital and the Coliseum site.

In line with its preservationist ideals, the M.A.S. has also targeted Columbus Circle as a tour area to show how development there can affect the neighborhood's light and how Central Park has influenced the development of the buildings around it. Both Barry Lewis and Michael George have led this tour.

Another M.A.S. tour visits the Hartley Settlement House on W. 46th Street, a brownstone, built circa 1850, which has been restored. An architect from the firm involved in the restoration discusses the structural details and the use of the building as housing for the poor.

In line with its purpose of focusing on currently important preservationist issues, the M.A.S. offers several tours of Times Square. Justin Ferate leads a walk called "Goodbye Times Square," which surveys the renovation of the area. So many old buildings have been torn down and new ones put up or scheduled to go up that the neighborhood in transition offers people a chance to see history-in-the-making. Another M.A.S.

tour tries to predict what Times Square will look like when it is filled with new office buildings in the year 2000.

The **Museum of Modern Art** is open daily except Wednesday, from 11:00 A.M. to 6:00 P.M. ; on Thursday evening it stays open until 9:00 P.M. and is free of charge to the public from 6:00 to 9:00 P.M. Guided group tours are available but must be arranged in advance. The museum sponsors daily free walks and tours to two or three galleries for visitors already in the museum. Talks vary in subject from day to day, from the highlights of current shows to specific art movements and artists. Visits to the permanent and changing collections are included.

The **Museum of the City of New York** has sponsored tours of the midtown Manhattan office-building area, beginning under the clock in the concourse of Grand Central Terminal and tracing the history of the development of the terminal's systems, from pre-World War I days, when the tracks were first covered, to the erection of Rockefeller Center in the 1930s. The tour lecture also discusses current architectural adventures in midtown.

The museum has another tour which visits the Garment District on Seventh Avenue in the West Thirties. Now a manufacturing zone, it was once a craft-oriented neighborhood. Milliners, lingerie manufacturers, and furriers are still concentrated there. Since so many Orthodox Jews were a part of the development of these crafts and of the Seventh Avenue clothing manufacturers' industry, you'll note several Orthodox synagogues, some with elaborately equipped arks and Torahs, serving each sector of the neighborhood's trades. (The W. 47th Street jewelry district, between Fifth and Sixth avenues, also the province of many Orthodox and Hasidic Jews, is a rather fascinating spectacle, from Monday through Friday noon. Tourists are urged to visit the street on their own, since the tour doesn't venture there—it's above 42nd Street.) The starting point for the Garment District walks is at Sixth Avenue and 34th Street, in front of Macy's.

The **N.B.C. Studios** offer guided tours daily, from 9:30 A.M. to 4:30 P.M.,

Mondays through Saturdays, and from 10:00 A.M. to 4:00 P.M., Sundays. Call 664–4000 to confirm the schedule. Tours, which leave the lobby of 30 Rockefeller Plaza, demonstrate how a network operates, visiting the set of the "Today Show," the newsrooms, and several other studios, too.

The **New York Public Library,** main branch, sponsors two walking tours of the library, free of charge to the public, Monday through Saturday at 11 A.M. and 2 P.M. The tour, which leaves from Astor Hall at the Fifth Avenue entrance, takes in the building's art and architecture as well as the collection of millions of books. On Monday through Saturday at 12:30 P.M., the library offers a tour of the current major exhibit in Gottesman Hall.

Henry Hope Reed, founder of Classical America, takes credit for leading the first walking tour of this magnificent building, which runs from 40th to 42nd streets on Fifth Avenue. Reed has written a meticulously detailed book about the library (The New York Public Library: Its Architecture and Decoration. New York: W. W. Norton, 1986). In it he discusses the library's founders: John Jacob Astor, Samuel J. Tilden, and James Lenox; Carrere & Hastings, the architectural firm that designed it; the halls, doorways, candelabra, and the head of Minerva—in short, the incredible richness of detail that constitutes the massive structure. Call 221–7676 for tour information and 930–0501 for group tours.

New York Walkabout takes groups to Roosevelt Island (originally called Blackwell's Island, after a prominent land-owning family) and discusses its metamorphosis from Welfare Island to the current, snug, suburban-style island community which bans automobile traffic from its streets.

See the sketch on Roosevelt Island on page 151 for a description of the island and the free-lance guides who take tour groups there.

Nikon House, at 620 Fifth Avenue, facing the Channel Gardens in Rockefeller Center, has a first-floor showroom and a second-floor booth where a Nikon camera repair person works on cameras brought by the public, in full view of a public audience, Tuesdays through Saturdays, from 10:00 A.M. to 5:45 P.M., free of charge. Call 586–3907 to confirm the schedule.

The **92nd Street "Y"** sponsors a variety of tours in midtown. One goes to Tudor City and the United Nations, beginning with the former, a large-scale urban-renewal project on the far east end of 42nd Street. This area, which is called Turtle Bay, possibly a reference to the turtles that lived there in Colonial days, had fallen into disrepute and disrepair in the twentieth century and needed a yeoman's effort to reclaim it from the tenements, gambling houses, stockyards, and slaughterhouses that had taken over. The tour moves uptown along First Avenue to the complex, stately United Nations Secretariat and General Assembly and many of the related buildings in the neighborhood, including 1 United Nations Plaza, a distinguished glass building housing offices, a health club, and a hotel.

Kate Simon, a well-known restaurant critic and author of *New York Places and Pleasures* (New York: Harper and Row, 1971), lives in the Kips Bay area of town, east of Murray Hill in the West Thirties. She leads a walk to show how the Levantine peoples have put their cultural and culinary stamps on the neighborhood's shops and restaurants.

Marvin Gelfand leads a "Y"-sponsored tour to the *New York Times* on W. 43rd Street to see the press and mechanical rooms as well as the third-floor newsroom, where many of the reporters and the editors for the daily edition work. The *Times* offices have been modernized from the days, prior to the 1970s, when the city room was a vast, barnlike space filled with simple desks and antiquated typewriters. Editors sat at one end, and reporters took up three-quarters of the remaining space, facing the metropolitan, national, and foreign news and copy-editing desks. Now the floors are carpeted and editors write on personal computers.

The tour also takes a nostalgic look at the nearby building on W. 41st Street where "Jock" Whitney's late-lamented *Herald Tribune* had its headquarters. The old tabloid, the *Daily Mirror,* also long gone, constitutes part of the itinerary, and so does *The New Yorker* Magazine at 25 W. 43rd Street. From there the group moves along Sixth Avenue to the Time-Life Building, part of Rockefeller Center's complex, at Sixth Avenue and W. 50th Street. Watering holes known and loved by editorial people are pointed out along the route.

The "Y" sponsors another midtown tour to the Jacob Javits Convention Center, designed by James Freed of I. M. Pei Partners. A member of the architectural firm delivers the lecture.

The Equitable Center constitutes another "Y" tour in midtown. With a striking, huge and colorful painting by Roy Lichtenstein on permanent display, the Seventh Avenue entrance to the building makes a very dramatic impression on visitors. The building has fourteen executive dining rooms, each one dedicated to a different American artist, with displays of their work. There also is a display of artist Brad Davis's work in an employees' dining room. The tour leader discusses the field of corporate art collecting. The Whitney Museum of Modern Art has a lobby-level exhibit annex here; it's open to the public, with changing exhibits.

The "Y" also sponsors tours to various midtown museums, including the Whitney Museum of American Art and the Museum of Modern Art.

The **Park Rangers** lead a variety of tours in that Olmsted and Vaux masterpiece of urban parkland design, Central Park, on regular schedules on weekends. Call 397–3080 to ascertain the changing topics and meeting points for the walks, which can vary widely in focus, from weather prediction to flora and fauna identification, to nature-photography techniques, identification of tree varieties, wreath making, crafts, astronomy (bring your own binoculars), dog handling, history lessons, animal studies, winter survival techniques, park-design theory, bird-feeding techniques, architecture around the park, map reading and compass use, Black History month, with visits to the Marcus Garvey and Duke Ellington monuments, and Ice Age remnants.

Radio City Music Hall schedules a tour every fifteen minutes from Monday through Saturday, with free admission for children under age six. You can reserve a tour for a group visit. The lecture covers the history of the art deco building, the pictures on the walls, even the stage elevators and the ladies' rooms, and all the artifacts and details of the theater.

Roosevelt Island is an out-of-the-way destination; relatively few tours reach it. To get there, you must take the tramway at 60th Street and Second Avenue, and on the other side you will find public shuttle service. Robin Lynn, coauthor with Margot Gayle of a book about Soho and Tribeca, leads tours of Roosevelt Island, where she lives. Gerard Wolfe includes the island, with its historic sites, in his repertoire of tours. Michael George occasionally visits this enclave, which is about two miles long and two-thirds of a mile wide.

The island, which was included in the Dutch Colonial settlement in the early seventeenth century, has had several names, one of which was Blackwell's Island, in honor of Robert Blackwell, a resident there in the late seventeenth and early eighteenth centuries. In the 1920s it became known as Welfare Island, because several institutions there catered to the city's indigent sick. A number of historic buildings, including the old Blackwell house, have been restored and preserved as part of the mid-twentieth-century Roosevelt Island Development, a village unto itself, with low-, middle-, and upper-income housing for about 5,000 families. No cars are allowed on the island. A bridge connects it to Ravenswood in Queens, and if the E. 63rd Street subway tunnel under the East River is ever completed, the island will have subway service to Manhattan proper. The lack of a subway has kept it a quaint suburb.

The **Seagram Building,** 375 Park Avenue at 53rd Street, designed by Ludwig Mies van der Rohe and Philip Johnson, constitutes an oasis in an overpowering landscape. Stand in front of the majestic Helmsley Building at 230 Park Avenue, which straddles the avenue at 46th Street, and look uptown at the sheer cliff-glass walls of the comparatively huge, newer office buildings. The Seagram Building, in contrast with these behemoths, is set back 90 feet from the street and has a graceful 27,000-square-foot plaza with fountains spraying glistening streams of water during the summer—altogether a study in the possible grace of minimalism. At midday in warm weather, the Seagram Building becomes a favorite picnic area for legions of midtown workers. The building spon-

151

sors a half-hour tour on Tuesdays at 3:00 P.M., free of charge, from the lobby to the fourth- and fifth-floor executive offices. Call 572–7000 to confirm the schedule.

John Tauranac's choices of interesting buildings to view in midtown constitute an edifying tour. Among the buildings that have caught his fancy enough for him to include in his book, *Essential New York* (Holt, Rinehart and Winston, 1979) are the Citicorp Building, Olympic Tower, Paley Park, St. Bartholomew's Church, the Ford Foundation, the Seagram Building, the Pan Am Building, the Galleria, Lever House, the United Nations, 1 United Nations Plaza, the *Daily News* Building, the Chrysler Building, the Waldorf Astoria, the University Club, the pretty, baroque Helmsley Building, which set the scale and tone for Park Avenue in the 1920s, and the Fred F. French Building, a classic example of setback architecture with tastefully ornate and glowing interior decoration and a polychromed terra-cotta exterior. Most of these East Side, midtown buildings, among the scores of buildings in his book, are within easy walking distance of each other and will provide you with an enlivening walk, even without Tauranac's presence as a leader. In his book, Tauranac has devised two separate walking-tour routes on Fifth Avenue and on the midtown streets and avenues to the east. The tours are easily combined.

The **United Nations** sponsors its own tours every day from 9:15 A.M. to 4:45 P.M., closing only on Christmas and New Year's Day, for everyone except children under age five. The sprawling complex that dominates midtown's Far East Side runs from E. 42nd Street to E. 48th Street along First Avenue, in Manhattan's Turtle Bay area. It is flanked by one of Manhattan's glamorous hotels—the United Nations Plaza at 1 U.N. Plaza—a swanky glass and chrome edifice whose bar is popular with United Nations personnel.

Joe Zito has given his Hell's Kitchen tour for colleges, local historical societies, and cultural institutions. A tall, rangy man in his mid-seventies, retired police captain Zito is one of the deans of the city guides. Though

152

he leads tours to several neighborhoods in Manhattan and Brooklyn, Hell's Kitchen is his favorite. He says that though the neighborhood is now called Clinton, because of its emerging upscale real-estate values, to him it will always be Hell's Kitchen, a legendary area, running roughly from West 34th Street to West 59th Street, from Eighth Avenue to the Hudson River. It was, and to some extent still is, a tough neighborhood. Zito knows plenty of tales, discourses knowledgeably about tenement architecture and laws, and points out the brownstone where George Washington Plunkett, a Tammany Hall district leader in the 1880s and '90s lived; Plunkett popularized the expression "honest graft," Joe Zito explains.

Another area Zito likes to visit is the former Tenderloin, now largely obliterated, which ran from about 24th to 34th streets and from Sixth to Eighth avenues. Now the commercial area south of Macy's, it was a seamy red-light and gambling district in the 1880s and 1890s—a role model for Hell's Kitchen.

Zito, who has a bachelor's degree in philosophy from Fordham University, lived most of his life in Brooklyn, but, because of his fascination with Hell's Kitchen's history and architecture, he and his family eventually moved there.

Chapter Eight

Upper West Side:
Morningside Heights,
Harlem, and Washington Heights

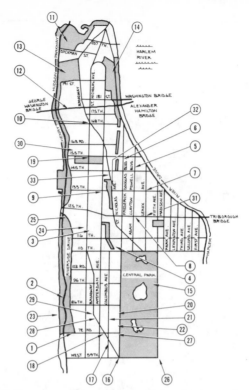

Points of Interest in the Upper West Side, Morningside Heights, Harlem, Inwood, and Washington Heights

1. Southern border of Riverside Park
2. Soldiers and Sailors Monument
3. Columbia University
4. Cathedral Church of St. John the Divine
5. Adam Clayton Powell Boulevard
6. Frederick Douglass Boulevard
7. The Schomburg Collection
8. The Apollo Theatre
9. City College of New York
10. Columbia University Medical Center
11. Inwood Hill Park
12. George Washington Bridge
13. Fort Tryon Park and the Cloisters
14. High Bridge Park
15. Central Park
16. Columbus Circle
17. Lincoln Center
18. Subway Kiosk
19. Hispanic Museum
20. Hayden Planetarium
21. American Museum of Natural History
22. New York Historical Society
23. Boat Basin
24. Barnard College
25. Grant's Tomb
26. Central Park South and the Plaza Hotel
27. The Dakota
28. Ansonia Hotel
29. Zabar's
30. Museum of the American Indian
31. Sylvia's Restaurant
32. Striver's Row (St. Nicholas Historic District)
33. Hamilton Heights Historic District

Of all the city's neighborhoods, the Upper West Side is the most hybrid, stretching from the grandeur of Lincoln Center's performance halls to W. 110th Street, the southern boundary of Columbia University's domain on Morningside Heights. (The Heights runs from approximately 110th Street to 125th Street.) In between those points, the Upper West Side reflects the entire history of the city's settlement, beginning most notably with the Dakota apartment building, at 1 W. 72nd Street, standing at the corner of Central Park West and taking up the block to 73rd Street.

Built in 1884, it was one of the first luxury apartment houses in Manhattan, and it prompted the wealthy to move from their private houses downtown to a veritable wilderness—the undeveloped Upper West Side. Late-nineteenth-century New Yorkers dubbed the building the Dakota because it seemed as remote to them as the Dakota territory. Originally, it had seven floors of apartments with four to twenty rooms each; the three top floors housed the servants' quarters and a children's playroom. The late John Lennon and his widow, Yoko Ono, bought many apartments in the building. Actress Lauren Bacall and former Mayor John V. Lindsay and his wife have been long-time residents. The building's architect, Henry J. Hardenbergh, was hired by the Singer-sewing-machine heir to build the Dakota for about one million dollars. The result was a building of formidably dark and stalwart mien, in neo-German Renaissance style, according to one description. There have been other technical and impressionistic descriptions of the building's style, too. Because of its forbidding stolidity, its costly cooperative apartments favored by celebrities, and its reputation as the setting for the film *Rosemary's Baby* and the murder of Beatle John Lennon, the Dakota has acquired greater mystique than any other glamorous residential building in town.

It helped set the tone for the development of the Upper West Side before and after the subway reached the area in 1904. Furthermore, as guide John Tauranac has pointed out, "It's almost axiomatic that population follows transportation." So the Upper West Side became a veritable boomtown, once the subway arrived. A neo-Dutch or Flemish Renaissance subway kiosk with baroque trimmings, one of three such landmark IRT control houses in Manhattan, was built on Broadway and 72nd Street, where it still stands.

Many prospering Jews and other immigrants as well as prominent entertainers, all finding their way up the economic ladder, moved into the neighborhood in the early years of the twentieth century. Actually these foreign, or nouveau riche, or eccentrically arty people, as the old-guard families of New York variously viewed them, were persona non grata on the Upper East Side. These newcomers had little choice but to flock to the Upper West Side. They made no apologies for their backgrounds and métiers. Performers loved the Ansonia Hotel, built in 1904, for its thick walls, which allowed them to practice in relative privacy, as well as for its hotel-style services. And the designs of many buildings reflected the newcomers' affinity for European style and panache—to the point of overdoing it. The Ansonia Hotel, for example, done in Beaux Arts style, is as ornate as a multitiered wedding cake.

It was placed on Broadway between 73rd and 74th streets, because Broadway was intented as New York's answer to Paris's *Champs Elysées*. To this day, the Upper West Side has maintained a vaguely foreign ambience, attractive to the newly famous, lately successful, and just-arrived immigrants from many countries—as well as to sophisticated, intellectual people from all types of backgrounds.

Anyone can feel comfortable in this melting pot, with its dashing hodgepodge of architecture, mélange of languages, potpourri of cuisines, and conglomeration of artists, professionals, upwardly mobile young couples and families, retirees, working poor, and abysmally nonworking poor. The restaurants there now have all the romance of the legendary Greenwich Village bistros.

Not the least of the Upper West Side's charms, emblematic of its trendiness, is Zabar's delicatessen on Broadway at 80th Street. It began as a kosher deli in Brooklyn, moved to the Upper West Side in the 1930s, and by the 1960s started to build its reputation as a gourmet deli, a veritable Jewish charcuterie.

Tour guides stress the architecture and the socioeconomic history of the Upper West Side. In the 1930s a number of art deco apartment houses—including the San Remo, the Majestic, the Eldorado, the Century and, to some extent, the Beresford were erected, inspired by the midtown Chrysler Building. They represent one aspect of the Upper West Side's architectural character. Guides such as Barry Lewis, who has given a pace-setting Upper West Side tour for the Municipal Art Society (and for other institutions as well), recounts when and how the Upper West Side developed, how it suffered through a decline in the mid-twentieth century, and then underwent a renaissance.

Some tours visit several of Manhattan's most notable sights—the Cathedral Church of St. John the Divine on Amsterdam Avenue at 112th Street, St. Luke's Hospital slightly to the north of the church, Columbia University's Beaux Arts main campus, running from Broadway to Amsterdam, flanking W. 116th Street, Morningside Park, and the Jewish Theological Seminary of America at Broadway and 122nd Street, a training ground for Conservative Jewish rabbis.

To the west of Broadway, within a few blocks of each other, are the Riverside Church, International House—a foreign students' residence—and Grant's Tomb, to name a few of the famous landmarks.

Across the street from St. John's on Amsterdam Avenue, the Hungarian Pastry Shop epitomizes the flavor of the neighborhood—and the

159

entire Upper West Side—as effectively as any one place for socializing possibly could. Here the Upper West Side's intellectuals gather for European-style coffees and pastries. Next door the Green Tree restaurant serves light meals. On dark nights, especially in summer, when the tables go outside, the Hungarian Pastry Shop is a brightly lit oasis, separating Columbia's campus from the predominantly Hispanic, low-income community which runs from about 110th Street down into the 90s.

From Morningside Heights, one can look down across Morningside Park, from the hilly Columbia neighborhood to Harlem. Though nearly a monolithic black community, Harlem is a district as varied culturally, socially, and economically as any other in town. It has acquired a reputation as a poor person's neighborhood, because of the rampant poverty, neglect, and crime there, but pockets of Harlem have become gentrified in the 1980s—and some areas have always maintained an aura of elegance. New and renovated apartment and office buildings suggest Harlem's economic fortunes are on the upswing on a wide scale. Not the least of Harlem's attractions are several relatively new cultural institutions, including the Studio Museum at 144 W. 125th Street, which features changing exhibits of the works of black artists and an educational and fellowship program; and the Schomburg Center for Research in Black Culture at 515 Lenox Avenue (renamed Malcom X Boulevard in 1988). The Schomburg Center has one of the largest existing collections of historic and cultural papers and artifacts relating to the black cultures of the United States, the Caribbean, and Africa.

An area of Harlem called Sugar Hill has always been known as an elegant and prestigious neighborhood. The Sugar Hill district runs from approximately 145th Street to 160th Street, between St. Nicholas and Edgecombe avenues. (By some estimates, Sugar Hill extends north approximately to 170th Street.) In any case, the most important apartment building in Sugar Hill, at 409 Edgecombe Avenue, has had some very important residents: Josh White, the folk singer, W. E. B. DuBois, and Roy Wilkins among them. And 555 Edgecombe Avenue, at 160th Street, was the home of Paul Robeson from 1949 to 1951. From 1956 to 1966 he lived at 16 Jumel Terrace, the site that most guides point out as Robeson's home. Duke Ellington lived at 935 St. Nicholas Avenue, just north of 155th Street, in the 1950s and '60s, and in the 1930s he lived at 381 Edgecombe Avenue. But 409 and 555 Edgecombe are two of the tallest buildings in the neighborhood, as well as two of the important, and on walking tours of Harlem you can keep them in view at all times. Not only has Lenox Avenue been renamed, but 125th Street has had an official name change to Martin Luther King, Jr. Boulevard. From 110th Street to 155th Street, Eighth Avenue is now Frederick Douglass Boulevard and Seventh Avenue is Adam Clayton Powell Boulevard.

A variety of bus and walking tours of Harlem have become established and popular—for Sunday-morning church services, for soul food, night life, cultural outings, and for views of historic houses. Harlem was once a German, then a Jewish, neighborhood and, long before all the ethnic groups arrived, a colonial outpost, traces of which remain. Several firms specialize in Harlem tours; many guides with expertise lead at least one tour similar to the route laid out in the thumbnail sketch of Justin Ferate's tour, described below.

North of Harlem, in a primarily Hispanic neighborhood, a notable museum, the Hispanic Society of America, at Broadway and W. 155th Street, exhibits the arts and cultures of Hispanic peoples, including paintings by Velasquez, Goya, and El Greco. Nearby stands the Museum of the American Indian. Also nearby is Columbia University's Medical Center and College of Physicians and Surgeons, with its main entrance facing Broadway between W. 165th and 168th streets. Columbia has other related medical and dental faculties and facilities in this neighborhood, which is actually the southern part of Washington Heights.

Venturing above the medical center, you reach the hilly, historic neighborhood known as Washington Heights, once the province of German-Jewish refugees, especially after World War II, and increasingly Hispanic these days. Here, near the northern tip of Manhattan, the colonists lost a battle to the British in 1776 and remained under British domination for several more years. Above Washington Heights and Fort Tryon Park, a popular recreation spot for neighborhood families on weekend days, you will reach Manhattan's northernmost community, Inwood, with its own park and community-sponsored walking tours. East of the park is Dyckman House, the only eighteenth-century Dutch

Upper West Side

Colonial farmhouse in Manhattan, between W. 204th and W. 207th streets. This restored historic landmark is open to the public on weekdays, a usual stop for walking tours in Manhattan's upper reaches.

Adventure on a Shoestring, an organization headed by Howard Goldberg, leads a yearly walk across the George Washington Bridge on October 25—the anniversary of the bridge's opening. The walk follows Interstate 195, a major highway, between W. 178th and W. 179th streets in Manhattan to Fort Lee, New Jersey, on a walkway on the bridge's upper level. The view on clear days is spectacular.

The American Museum of Natural History sponsors a variety of tours led by many members of the museum's staff. Best known as a walking-tour guide, within the museum, on its grounds, and sometimes in Central Park and in other parts of town, geologist Dr. Sidney Horenstein has a special flair for lectures and tours. He puts to rest the notion that you can't get blood out of a stone, because under his tutelage, with the natural urban landscape as his inspiration, he makes history and the people who lived in past eras come alive.

He discusses the ways in which people altered New York's landscape by constructing parks and streets and how the legacy reflects the various periods in which people lived. He looks at the geology of buildings and discusses the history of stone-building techniques, architectural uses of stone, and how it weathers and disintegrates.

At the museum, Horenstein leads people around the massive granite building (horses and carriages collapsed trying to transport materials for its construction), explaining how the building is disintegrating, with stalactites forming from the stone at the southern entrance. He also calls attention to the differences in temperature between the sunken entranceway and the higher ground a few feet above.

He describes the sources and types of stone used for the building's original construction and additions, and he circumnavigates the building, talking about the stones, trees, and sculptures in the museum's park, examining how they have withstood or succumbed to the ravages of nature and vandalism.

After about an hour's stroll, he re-enters the building, at its main entrance facing Central Park West, and explains the history of the imposing entrance hall. Its murals pay tribute to the sportsman/huntsman, President Theodore Roosevelt. The architect for the project was John Russell Pope, who won the state-sponsored competition for the Theodore Roosevelt Memorial Hall. In the hall, which is of ornate, classical design, Horenstein talks about the composition of the rich marble walls and floor and eventually hikes through several galleries, teaching people about limestone and marble, of which much of the building is made, describing how the stones were formed. He points out the tiny fossils clearly imbedded in the stones and instructs people how to recognize the differences between marble and other stones. His explanation of the ways in which they were formed during the millenia of the earth's evolution is exciting, especially while people view the delicate-looking handiwork of the tumultuous forces of nature.

"Wild Man" Steve Brill leads tours that are independent of the Park Ranger's walks, for his focus is different from the usual naturalist tours. He takes people into Central Park and points out edible plants, herbs, and mushrooms, gives people the information necessary to identify them by themselves, and provides tips on safety and the best methods of picking these wild plants. He takes about twenty people on his walks in various city parks every Saturday and Sunday, from 11:45 A.M. to 3:45 P.M., between March and December. The Central Park walk takes place once every three weeks. Mr. Brill also does a berry-picking tour on bicycle and leads walking tours in Inwood, Riverside, and Fort Tryon parks.

Not all, but most, of his Central Park walks begin at the 72nd Street–Central Park West entrance. It's a good idea, even in the hottest weather, to wear long-sleeved shirts and long pants, to protect your skin from mosquitoes, gnats, poison ivy, and twigs; alternatively, cover yourself thoroughly with insect repellent. Mr. Brill will tell you what types of bags to bring for your food-picking.

He, too, is a guide blessed with a gift for entertaining while lecturing, and his enthusiasm and nimbleness as he runs up and down hills in pursuit of his quarry are both infectious and impressive. He has been seen in a state of excitement when discovering a particular type of dogwood: "This is a first for Central Park!" he calls out. As for cat briar, or green briar, which he instructs you to put in salads, he says, "It's one of my favorite green vegetables." You will get to see and sample wild onions; poor man's pepper; wild raisins that taste like prune butter (in October); and white and red mulberries (in June). Brill brings along a drop cloth; everyone joins in shaking berries off the trees.

Nobody is supposed to shake trees in Central Park except on Brill's tours, he tells you, but you can go to an abandoned railroad bed north of the George Washington Bridge and shake the trees there legally. No matter what time of year you go along with him, you'll always find some items in bloom—and others out of season. "If every berry were edible now, we'd all go nuts," he says philosophically to his groups. June berries, related to apples, are exceptionally good in early summer, while hawthorne berries are a treat in September. Venturing off the beaten paths to virtually hidden streams in Central Park, he uncovers such items as huge, saddle mushrooms, which he tells people how to cook.

Columbia University offers several walking tours every year through its "Encore Series," which is open to the public. The walks are led by Columbia University history professor Dr. James P. Shenton. He instituted his first walking tour about fifteen years ago under the school's auspices for a nineteenth-century American history course dealing with the city's 1863 draft riots. Since then, for his courses, the university, and other cultural and educational institutions and groups, this stellar guide has led groups to many neighborhoods in all the boroughs.

At Columbia, he escorts people around the Beaux Arts campus, designed by McKim, Mead and White in the 1890s. The tour includes the American ceramics collection in Low Library. He also visits Grant's Tomb, the Interfaith Center, Riverside Church, Barnard College, the Cathedral Church of St. John the Divine—"If you want to know how to build a Gothic Cathedral, you'll see how it's done," he explains—and the

Jewish Theological Seminary at 122nd Street and Broadway.

His Upper West Side tour surveys the area's diversity—"a classic example of what everyone thinks the city is about," he says. He remarks on the many unmarked borders that exist on the Upper West Side, particularly from 85th Street to 100th streets, and along Columbus Avenue—much like those that exist in Los Angeles—and notes: "Everyone is startled by the abrupt changes in the area." He always ends his walks at Zabar's.

Shenton also leads tours of Harlem, sometimes beginning on Morningside Drive on the Heights, looking down into Harlem, from 100th to 125th streets. Another route takes him past the Apollo Theatre on 125th Street to Lenox Avenue or sometimes to St. Nicholas Avenue, then to Striver's Row, also called the St. Nicholas Historic District: four rows of fine, late-nineteenth-century residences along 138th and 139th streets, built in neo-Georgian and neo-Italian Rennaissance style for the neighborhood's well-to-do, who wanted a peaceful enclave within the city. Walking downtown, observing the street life, Shenton ends this tour at Sylvia's, a well-known soul-food restaurant on Lenox Avenue (Malcom X Boulevard) between 126th and 127th streets.

Another Shenton tour focuses on Harlem's "upper west side," with a visit to Hamilton Grange, once the summer home of Alexander Hamilton, at 287 Convent Avenue between 141st and 142nd streets, now maintained by the National Park Service. Built in 1801, the house was moved from a nearby site to its present address in 1889; in the process its front and rear porches were removed. Before the house received its landmark status, it served as a chapel and a rectory.

Shenton's tours vary in price, depending upon whether he directs walks for Columbia University or other sponsors.

Columbia University also offers walking tours as part of courses in the architectural history of New York City from Dutch Colonial farmhouses to postmodern skyscrapers. Course prices are in the neighborhood of $1,000 each, skyscrapers in themselves (the quintessence of "higher" education). Tour leaders are Professors Andrew Dolkart and Donald Reynolds.

Justin Ferate, known as a Brooklyn specialist, is also an adept guide in many Manhattan neighborhoods, including Harlem.

On a three-hour tour there, Ferate begins at Park Avenue and 125th Street (Martin Luther King, Jr., Boulevard), near the elevated train. It symbolizes the fact that Harlem's development was a side effect of the economic impact of the N. Y. Central Railroad. From there he walks to the old Harlem Courthouse, 170 E. 121st Street, at Sylvan Terrace, built in the 1890s, in Victorian Gothic style, with late Romanesque features, including terra-cotta. The courthouse functioned within the legal system until the 1960s. Now it's a Department of Environmental Protection office.

Across the street from the courthouse, Ferate points out seven simple but charming brick townhouses on a residential walkway, Sylvan Court, and the Elmendorf Reformed Church. This is the oldest Harlem congregation, dating to the early 1900s, and a successor to a 1660 Dutch church there. He wends his way to Madison Avenue and thereafter zigzags between Madison and Fifth avenues, to see churches and row houses, including All Saints Roman Catholic Church and a house that belonged at one time to the heavyweight boxing champion, Jack Johnson, and later to Father Divine. "It has a gorgeous porch that looks like Valentine lace," says Mr. Ferate. "It points itself out."

On 127th Street, between Madison and Fifth, he visits the house of poet Langston Hughes and from there proceeds to the 130th Street row houses, with front porches and yards, between Fifth and Lenox avenues. Though a little bedraggled now, they are landmark houses and are especially interesting for the Stars of David over their doors, connoting that Ethiopian Jews, or Felashas, have settled here.

Ferate swings left along Lenox Avenue and passes Sylvia's restaurant, on the east side of Lenox, heading south to Marcus Garvey Park between 121st and 124th streets. From there the tour proceeds to several Lenox Avenue churches, crosses 125th Street, and visits Theresa Towers, an office building that replaced the old Hotel Theresa. Outside of Harlem it is probably best known for its famous guest, Fidel Castro, who stayed there in the early 1960s when he visited the United Nations. The tour stops at the Studio Museum of Harlem, takes a peek at the

Amsterdam News on Frederick Douglass Boulevard (formerly Eighth
Avenue), then heads down St. Nicholas Avenue to Hancock Park, named
in the 1890s for a presidential contender, and to the site of the former
Harlem Opera House, built by Oscar Hammerstein on 125th Street. An
amateur hour originally held the opera house eventually moved to the
Apollo Theatre; many leading black musicians won contests and
launched their careers there. Contrary to popular belief, Ella Fitzgerald
won the amateur contest in the opera house, not the Apollo Theatre
proper.

Continuing west on 125th Street, the tour arrives at St. Joseph's
Church, heads up a hill to the site of a former brewery, and after visiting
a few more historic sites, ends at the IRT subway station, at Broadway
and 125th Street, with its imposing viaduct dating back to about 1904.

This route through Harlem is popular with many tour leaders.

Friends of Inwood Park has developed a walking-tour program. Veteran botanist Bill Greiner (942-2450) has been leading these tours since
1970. (It should be noted that many city parks have "Friends of" organizations.) Friends of Inwood Park has also asked historians and geologists
to lead its monthly tours occasionally, except in very cold weather.
"Wild Man" Steve Brill leads tours here, too. Tours take place on the last
Sunday in the month at 1:00 P.M. The meeting place is the flagpole by
the tennis court, at Isham Street (208th Street).

Friends of Fort Tryon Park, to the south, has a more casual approach to walking tours, which are sponsored only occasionally. "Wild
Man" Steve Brill also leads tours there.

Marvin Gelfand's Walk of the Town features Upper West Side and
Harlem tours that sometimes stretch out longer than their scheduled
two hours. On the Upper West Side, Gelfand takes many routes and
makes myriad excursions into churches and synagogues, as he delivers
narratives about famous writers, lovers, entertainers, socialites, politicians, and other prominent figures who have lived in the area. He also
talks about famous crimes that have taken place there, such as the
"Looking for Mr. Goodbar" murder.

Upper West Side

Here's the itinerary for his Riverside Drive tour. He begins at a mansion where artist Marc Chagall lived, proceeds to the house where George and Ira Gershwin had a double penthouse, then walks to 137 Riverside Drive at 86th Street, where William Randolph Hearst lived, with a collection of very valuable art and artifacts. Gelfand points out Mount Tom, a rock outcropping at 83rd Street, where Edgar Allan Poe used to sit and scribble. Other houses of note along the Drive—either for their architecture, or their famous residents past and present—are stops on the tour; neighborhood residents have included actress Ruth Gordon, gangster Arnold Rothstein, writer Heywood Broun, Nobel Prize-winner Isaac Bashevis Singer (who still lives in the Belnord on 86th Street), and Damon Runyon.

In Harlem, where Gelfand is one of the few specialists on the traces of Jewish history, he visits the house where Richard Rodgers was born at 120th Street and Mt. Morris Park West, and the Regent Movie House, once directed by Roxy (who later directed the famous midtown theater, the Roxy). The Regent is now the First Corinthian Baptist Church at 116th Street and Seventh Avenue (Adam Clayton Powell Boulevard). A family named Schiffman bought the Apollo Theatre and turned it into an integrated house in 1934; it made the Schiffmans entertainment barons and created a legendary theater in the history of American entertainment.

Michael George, leading tours for Classical America, New York University, and various cultural institutions and groups, counts Morningside Heights as one of his favorite areas. It began to blossom in the 1890s with the arrival of the Cathedral Church of St. John the Divine, Columbia University's Beaux Arts campus, and St. Luke's Hospital—three major groups of buildings designed by prominent architects clearly intent upon creating important statements.

McKim, Mead and White helped to design Columbia University; Heins and LaFarge, and Cram & Ferguson designed St. John's; while Ernest Flagg of Flagg & Chambers planned St. Luke's, an innovative hospital designed to provide plenty of fresh air and space for patients.

The Cathedral Church was placed on the crest of a hill, where it would be the dominant force in the landscape.

Val Ginter's Ginter-Gotham Urban History has several Upper West Side and Harlem tours. One Ginter tour in Harlem, one of his specialties, parallels Justin Ferate's. Ginter, who formerly played jazz accordion professionally, has created his own "History of Jazz in New York" tour, including the following sites: Edwin E. Smalls' South Carolina Sugar Cane club; the Savoy Ballroom, where big bands had contests to see which was the greatest of them all, during the Big Band era; the Cotton Club at Lenox Avenue near 143d Street; Clark Monroe's Uptown House, where Charlie Parker and Dizzy Gillespie worked out their revolutionary style of music, bebop, in the 1940s, and which now has a Monroe Shock Absorber sign in the window; Connie's Inn at 2221 Seventh Avenue (Adam Clayton Powell Boulevard), where Fats Waller loved to while away his time and tip a few drinks to his Muse; Dickie Wells's club, a block away from Monroe's; the Joe Louis Bar; the Lionel Hampton Houses; and Small's Paradise at 2294 Adam Clayton Powell Boulevard at 135th Street.

Scott Joplin, W. C. Handy, Eubie Blake, Noble Sissle, and Fletcher Henerson, all composers and jazz musicians, lived on Striver's Row, so it's a stop on a Ginter tour as well as on his neighborhood tours. The Fletcher Henderson townhouse, where the great Big Band leader lived, at 224 W. 139th Street, and Duke Ellington's house at 386 Riverside Drive, are included on tours, too. So is Minton's Playhouse, at 208 W. 118th Street, the other Harlem club where Parker and Gillespie and their colleagues worked out revolutionary embellishments of modern jazz. The Alhambra, Lincoln, Lafayette, and Apollo theaters are points of interest, too, for jazz fans.

Ginter's jazz tour includes the Abyssinian Baptist Church, where the funerals of Parker, tenor saxophonist Harold Vick, and Count Basie were held (and were mobbed by the public). On occasion, Ginter also heads downtown to the Riverside Church from 120th to 122nd streets on Riverside Drive, the Cathedral Church of St. John the Divine at Amsterdam Avenue and 112th Street (Cathedral Parkway), which has had historic jazz performances, and the Church of the Heavenly Rest at Fifth Avenue and 90th Street, technically below Harlem but also a sponsor of many exciting jazz performances.

Ginter's repertoire also includes a tour of Morningside Heights and another walk from Central Park West to Riverside Drive. The latter concentrates on the Dakota-Ansonia area in the West Seventies. Ginter can also tour Washington Heights from 155th Street to 187th Street, visiting the sites of the Audubon Ballroom, Audubon Terrace, the wooden row houses of Jumel Terrace, and the Morris-Jumel Mansion— the only surviving pre-Revolutionary house in Manhattan. It was built in 1765–66 as the county seat of Colonel Roger Morris. Later it was purchased by a French wine merchant, Stephen Jumel. His intriguing, life-loving widow married an elderly Aaron Burr and outlived him, too, for more than forty years. The tour also passes the United Church (Rev. Ike's church), once a Loew's movie theater, and a nineteenth-century Romanesque water tower in Highbridge Park. Ginter followed this route for a Municipal Art Society-sponsored tour far from the beaten path and madding crowd of midtown, ending in front of the former Paterno Guest House, at 186th Street and Chittenden Avenue.

Harlem Spirituals, Inc. leads a bus tour on Sunday mornings, leaving from the Short Line Office, 166 W. 46th Street, between Sixth and Seventh avenues, at 8:45 A.M., primarily for a visit to a Baptist church to hear spirituals and gospel music. You must call to reserve a place.

The firm also sponsors bus tours to Harlem during the week. These take you to 125th Street, Harlem's main street, for shopping, as well as to the Liberation Bookstore, Hamilton Grange, Aunt Len's Doll and Toy Museum, the Morris-Jumel Mansion, and a restaurant. Tours leave at 9:00 A.M. and conclude about 1:30 P.M., after lunch at either Wilson's Restaurant at 158th Street and Madison Avenue or at Singleton's Barbecue, Lenox Avenue at 136th Street.

On weekend nights, the firm sponsors jazz-and-restaurant tours. For this type of tour, Sylvia's, a well-known soul-food restaurant, is on the agenda, and the list of clubs includes the Baby Grand, the Showman, and Billy's. The itinerary is subject to change.

Harlem, Your Way! Tours Unlimited, Inc. offers a variety of tours, including a daily walking tour, and several classes in Harlem. The daily walking tour visits the Liberation Bookstore on Lenox Avenue, the Schomburg Center, the Abyssinian Baptist Church and its Rev. Adam Clayton Powell, Jr., Memorial Room (Powell was the country's first black congressman), and continues down Striver's Row to Hamilton Heights. For clients who request it, Aunt Len's Doll and Toy Museum is a stop. There's a tiny entrance fee there, as there is at the Schomburg Center. The walk goes on to the Theresa Towers, once a hotel; Marcus Garvey Park; Sylvia's and La Famille restaurants; City College; 125th Street's Apollo Theatre and Baby Grand Club; the Handmaids of Mary Convent—an all-black convent; and ends at the Studio Museum.

Other tours or additions to the daily walking tour involve visits to the Jumel Mansion, the Museum of the American Indian, and Sylvan Terrace.

A gospel tour is given on Sunday mornings at 10:30. Tourists meet at the firm's headquarters in an 1882 brownstone with an art gallery. A black-history walk through Harlem, including a slide show, ends at a soul-food restaurant. The firm also takes tourists on a photography lesson/walking tour of the neighborhood. A brownstone walking tour is another of this firm's specialties. Once a year, too, the firm sponsors a brownstone workshop, teaching people how to buy brownstones, with information on legalities, financing, repairs, and renovations. Groups can also take evening tours, beginning with a champagne cocktail at the firm's offices, proceeding to a local club, or, on Wednesday nights, the revived Amateur Night at the Apollo Theatre.

Arthur Marks, who created the walking-tour program for the New-York Historical Society, also leads independent tours of the Upper West Side—for example, to the Columbia University-Morningside Heights area, to visit Grant's Tomb, Riverside Church, the Cathedral Church of St. John the Divine, and the Eglise de Notre Dame (Church of Our Lady), whose dome reminds Mr. Marks of The Pantheon.

The Municipal Art Society sponsors tours of neighborhoods or specific buildings in all the boroughs. In 1988 the M.A.S. planned a tour to call attention to residential development in Harlem. The route included Central Park's northern border, 110th Street (Cathedral Parkway), Towers on the Park, a condominium project, the rental building Graham Court, poet Langston Hughes' former home, and Striver's Row. The tour and accompanying lecture reflected the M.A.S.'s concern with affordable housing.

Barry Lewis, the guide's guide, has led a jewel of a tour for the M.A.S. (as well as for many others) on the newly gentrified Upper West Side. Taking a route that zig-zagged through only a few blocks, from 72nd Street and Central Park West, the Dakota's site, to Broadway near the Ansonia Hotel, Mr. Lewis discourses for three hours on the development of apartment and row houses—and, by association, the development of life-styles and social and economic classes in New York City during the past century. Among Mr. Lewis's insights on this tour: "New York never changes except that the scale becomes much bigger."

Lewis recounts the metamorphosis of the Upper West Side from a dangerous, neglected neighborhood after World War II to an expensive trendy neighborhood currently. Lewis also explains why the West Side has fewer avenues than the East Side: The corner properties were the most valuable; the more corners, the more valuable property available. On the Upper East Side, the wealthier part of town, it seemed reasonable to have more corners. And the greater number of avenues on the Upper East Side made it lighter and airier than the West Side.

The Museum of the City of New York schedules an Upper West Side tour as part of its regular spring and fall walks. The lecture covers much of the same territory as Lewis's tour concerning residential development: row housing, tenement housing near public transportation, and luxury apartment living in buildings such as the Dakota, the Belnord, the Apthorp, and the Ansonia and their impact on the apartment in the city's social history. The tour starts at the Dakota.

The museum also leads a tour of Harlem, beginning on the steps of the museum's building at 103rd Street and Fifth Avenue. The lecture delves back into Harlem's days as a colonial farm village linked to downtown Manhattan by a wagon road built by slaves of the Dutch West India Company. By the 1920s Harlem had become America's largest black community, because of migration from other parts of the city, the South, and the West Indies. The tour visits Harlem churches, cultural institutions, and restaurants; looks for traces of the world-famous culture of Harlem in the 1920s, during the Jazz Age and the Harlem Renaissance; and examines the neighborhood's current struggle to progress.

The Washington Heights tour led by the museum focuses on the influx of Dominican and Puerto Rican immigrants, who dominate much of the neighborhood, with their ethnic institutions, stores, houses, churches, and social services as well as unprotected sweatshops. This tour begins at the southeast corner of Cathedral Parkway (W. 110th Street) and Broadway.

The New-York Historical Society begins its tour of the Upper West Side at Lincoln Center's plaza, in front of the Metropolitan Opera House, near W. 63rd Street. On the plaza, the tour group hears a lecture on the area's development, including such structures as the Empire Hotel, the Society for Ethical Culture, and Lincoln Center itself. Many of the opening shots for the movie *West Side Story* were taken from the site of Lincoln Center. The film's action took place in a tenement neighborhood nearby, which has been replaced by Lincoln Towers.

The tour heads up Broadway. At 66th Street, people are reminded that Campbell's Funeral Home was the site of a riot during film star Rudolph Valentino's funeral in the 1920s. The group pauses to look up Broadway to the Ansonia Hotel. The lecture encompasses the development of the Upper West Side's transportation and housing in the late nineteenth and early twentieth centuries. At 70th Street, the group heads east, passing the Pythian Temple, an exotic, ornately designed building with an interesting motto on its art deco facade: "If fraternal love held all men bound, how beautiful this world would be." The temple is now an expensive cooperative apartment house.

The tour continues to Temple Shéarith Israel, the oldest congregation of New York City's Jewish community. Heading north on Central

Park West, the group glimpes the Dakota, the Majestic, the San Remo, the Dorralton, and other apartment houses. Since every tour guide puts his or her own stamp on his lecture, it's not surprising to hear one of the guides for the groups of The New-York Historical Society describe the Dakota as "a grotesque parody of French Second Empire."

After entering Central Park for a glimpse of Strawberry Fields, the memorial built by Yoko Ono for her assassinated husband, John Lennon, the group continues to the Universalist Church, the American Museum of Natural History, and ends with a reception at The New-York Historical Society on Central Park West.

The 92nd Street "Y" rotates its tours, offering some walks one year, other popular destinations another year, sometimes scheduling one-of-a-kind, one-time-only walks, too. So each season you must contact the "Y" for its latest lineup. Marvin Gelfand has led tours of Jewish Harlem for the "Y." These tours usually visit the former homes of the Sulzbergers, who founded the *New York Times,* and other prominent, wealthy Jewish families, and those of theater people such as Richard Rodgers, Lorenz Hart, and Arthur Miller, and of writer Nathaniel West, author of *Day of the Locust* and *Miss Lonelyhearts.* The tours may also make the rounds of old synagogues, row houses, and theaters of significance to the Jewish community.

Val Ginter created a river-to-river walk on 125th Street, Harlem's "Main Street," for the "Y." Recently, Justin Ferate has been leading a similar tour. In its "Behind the Scenes" series, featuring tours with novel destinations, the "Y" included "An Evening at the Apollo," the renovated 125th Street theater that served as a showcase for some of the country's greatest entertainers, many of them black. The theater's lobby is now decorated with photographs of its illustrious past. Famous entertainers still perform here on an irregular basis. Witnessing current productions from a high balcony seat, you may begin to imagine the awed feelings of the new entertainers who, on amateur nights, trembled to confront Harlem's demanding audiences. Inept youngsters were booed offstage summarily.

The Park Rangers, in addition to their tours of Central Park at many points between its 59th Street and 110th Street borders (see page 12), schedules tours of the Upper West Side and of other parks in upper Manhattan. The topics at Inwood Hill Park include hawks, and, the Park Rangers suggest alluringly, perhaps even a bald eagle. Bring your binoculars to the flagpole by the Isham Street and Seaman Avenue entrance, the usual starting point for most tours of this park. The Rangers also teach nature photography and Manhattan geology here.

At Hamilton Grange they discuss the lives and times of Alexander Hamilton and Aaron Burr. The tour meets at 141st Street and St. Nicholas Avenue.

In Morningside Park, the Rangers discuss the design of the terraces and parapets created by Olmsted and Vaux, who also designed Central Park. The tour starts at Cathedral Parkway (W. 110th Street) and Morningside Drive.

In Riverside Park, beginning at 106th Street and Riverside Drive, the Rangers give lessons in tree identification and animal and plant life in the park.

In Fort Tryon Park, the Rangers also lead groups to see geological traces of the city's past, including the Ice Age. Tours start at the Unicorn Café.

You must check with the Park Rangers' office, because these specialty tours, among 700 to 800 led annually by the Rangers, are given on an irregular schedule.

Pete Salwen, author of a new book on the Upper West Side, (Abbeville Press), has led tours that last as long as four hours, from 72nd Street to 123rd Street along Riverside Drive. From Salwen, you will learn that a banker named Cyrus Clark bought a house in the West Nineties overlooking Riverside Park as early as 1866. He tried to encourage development in the area, and there's a memorial to him hidden in the park.

When Pete Salwen was growing up on W. 89th Street, he became fascinated in 1970 by the Soldiers and Sailors Monument on 89th Street and Riverside Drive. Sculpted by Paul E. Duboy in 1902 and modeled after the Choragic Monument of Lysicrates in Athens, Greece, the monument was given a grand setting with plenty of steps to honor the soldiers and sailors of the Civil War. By the time Salwen finished studying the monument, he was "obsessed with New York City," he recalls.

He majored in antropology at Cornell University, then returned to New York City to continue his studies of the city. He has read six volumes of *The Iconography of Manhattan Island*, by I. N. P. Stokes, whose uncle built the Ansonia Hotel. Salwen has also written articles on the Upper West Side, while collecting material for his own book.

His tour begins on W. 72nd Street, a fine residential street in the 1890s; he points out two limestone-fronted, turn-of-the-century "chateaus" on this now busy commercial street, then heads to Riverside Park, where he discusses the positive and negative aspects of the park's design by Frederick Law Olmsted and others. Proceeding up Riverside Drive, with mini-excursions into side streets, he visits some impressive pre- and postwar (World War II) apartment houses, including 33 Riverside Drive at the northeast corner of 75th Street, where George and Ira Gershwin had adjoining penthouses during the Jazz Age. Lillian Russell lived nearby in the 1890s at 318 W. 77th Street.

Among other important apartment houses, the Normandie, between 86th and 87th streets on Riverside Drive, is singled out. Its architect, Emery Roth, also designed the venerable Beresford and San Remo apartment houses on Central Park West. Salwen also passes by the 87th Street Viaduct, the Soldiers and Sailors Monument, and Yeshiva Chofetz Chaim (originally the mansion of Isaac L. Rice, a prominent lawyer whose wife founded the Society for the Suppression of Unnecessary Noise, a forerunner of the futile attempts of the Department of Environmental Protection to this day). Joan of Arc Park, running from 92nd to 95th streets, has a statue of the saint. An undulating section called the Upper Drive, from 97th to 113th streets, intended for private mansions, now contains the Firemen's Memorial at 100th Street, and, at 105th Street, a historic block of Beaux Arts townhouses built between 1899 and 1902. One was bought by William Randolph Hearst for his mistress, Marion Davies. Duke Ellington lived in another. In fact, 106th Street is named for Ellington.

Other high points of the tour are the Equestrian Monument at 106th

Street and the Children's Mansion at 107th Street, at one time a girls' finishing school, later a day-care center, designed by architect William B. Tuthill, who designed Carnegie Hall. At 319 W. 107th Street, the Nicholas Roerich Museum is open to the public, displaying the works and collections of this expatriate Russian artist, writer, scenarist, explorer, and mystic. Not the least of the townhouse's charms is its interior design.

Above 110th Street, the tour notes the Samuel J. Tilden statue at 112th Street; the curved apartment houses at Riverside Drive and 116th Street leading up a graceful hill to Columbia University's campus; the Interchurch Center at 475 Riverside Drive at 120th Street; the Riverside Church, modeled after Chartres Cathedral; Grant's Tomb; the Amiable Child Memorial, commemorating a child who drowned accidentally in the late eighteenth century; and International House, a residence for foreign students in New York City, at 500 Riverside Drive.

Joseph L. Schiff, head of Jewish Urban Study Tours, leads a tour called "Marjorie Morningstar Is Alive and Well and Back on West End Avenue." He points out such highlights as the Temple Shéarith Israel, successor to the first Spanish-Portuguese synagogue in New York City's historic financial district. Schiff also traces the migration and history of the Jews on the Upper West Side. He tells how the Dakota preceded the synagogue to the Upper West Side by about ten years. Jews, who were prospering on the Lower East Side, moved uptown to the Upper West Side in considerable numbers, creating an innovative, sophisticated Jewish community in an area where they felt welcome. The Upper East Side did not want them, and though that situation has altered radically in this century, many Jews still remain on the Upper West Side. They practice all forms of Judaism, from Hasidism to Reconstructionism, with synagogues ranging from the Orthodox to the counterculture. Schiff also leads a tour of "The World of Modern Orthodoxy" at Yeshiva University in Washington Heights, and another tour of the Conservative Jewish Theological Seminary on Broadway at 122nd Street.

Schiff graduated with a degree in sociology from City College of New York, then spent two years in the School of Judaica at the Jewish Theological Seminary. He's a former director of the West Side Jewish

Community Council and an Upper West Side resident. And he regards his métier of giving people an education in Jewish history, culture, and religion in the city streets as "a combination of scholarship, entertainment, and traffic management," he says.

Ron Spence, a free-lance guide who conducts all the tours for a firm called Harlem Renaissance, was born and brought up in Harlem, where he still lives. He also conducts tours for several other travel and tourism-industry firms and for schools.

One of his favorite tours begins at the Riverside Church, at Riverside Drive and 120th to 122nd streets, where he takes groups to the bell tower for a view of the entire city. From there he goes to the Cathedral Church of St. John the Divine, walks up Amsterdam Avenue, crosses Columbia University's campus, to Broadway, goes back to Riverside Drive and the church, up to Grant's Tomb, and then to 125th Street and Broadway. Then he proceeds up Convent Avenue to City College and continues to 145th Street, where he points out several major sights: townhouses and brownstones at Convent Avenue and Hamilton Terrace, once the summer home of Alexander Hamilton, and the Roman Catholic church, Our Lady of Lourdes, at 467 W. 142nd Street, just outside the Hamilton Heights Historic District, built in 1902–1904. Spence also points out the Convent Avenue Baptist Church at 145th Street. He explains to people that they are entering Harlem's Sugar Hill section, where many celebrities once lived, in some fine buildings. Sugar Hill starts at 145th Steet and continues to 160th Street or even further north by some estimates, and contains Edgecombe Avenue on the East and, to the west, Convent and then Amsterdam avenues. St. Nicholas Avenue, part of the old Boston Post Road, cuts through this section.

For another route, he proceeds from 125th Street up Seventh Avenue to Striver's Row, then crosses to St. Nicholas Avenue, heads to Hamilton Heights and Sugar Hill, pointing out with particular pride the mystique of the area which, in his view, symbolizes the spirit and raison d'être for the Harlem renaissance now underway.

John Tauranac, urban architectural historian, writer, teacher, and M.T.A. consultant, leads an Upper West Side tour from Columbus Circle to the Apthorp Apartments at 79th Street and Broadway—in his view, a "baroque extravaganza." Tauranac notes that the Upper West Side has a rich architectural diversity, with something worth looking at on every block. Between 59th Street, where the tour begins, and its 79th Street finishing point, he zigs and zags through the side streets, choosing a variety of sites around which he weaves a history of the neighborhood's development and views every architectural style in town from 1884 to the present.

He also likes to lead a tour from the Cathedral Church of St. John the Divine to Grant's Tomb on Morningside Heights, including Columbia's campus, St. Luke's Hospital, and a Leake & Watts building, once used as an orphanage, done in French Revival style, south of St. John's. He also views apartment buildings along Claremont Avenue and Riverside Drive, which were erected after the subway started serving the neighborhood in 1904.

Chapter Nine

Brooklyn, the Bronx, Queens, and Staten Island

Something magical happens when you cross into Manhattan from the four other boroughs that have made up the city of New York since 1898. Right away you can sense the dynamism, the fast pace, the effervescence of the crowds. Some Manhattanites have barely peeked at any of the outer boroughs, because, with only some degree of truth, the Big Apple's career-oriented population regards the neighboring boroughs as bastions of middle-class family life. And many Manhattanites have transplanted themselves from other parts of the country precisely for the glamor in Manhattan.

But millions of people know that something charming also happens when you leave Manhattan and visit or live in the boroughs. They're quieter, cleaner, and airier than Manhattan, and some sections are prettier, with less street crime. All the boroughs have historic districts with distinguished examples of Colonial, eighteenth-, and nineteenth-century architecture; there have always been some people who have preferred the outskirts of the main settlement, for a variety of reasons. As testimony, in Flushing, Queens, at 137-16 Northern Boulevard, between Main and Union streets, stands an austere Quaker Meeting House built between 1694 and 1717—one of the oldest buildings standing in New York City. So for architecture and history buffs, the boroughs can provide exciting walking tours.

People looking for diversity of life-styles within New York City's

182

borders are delighted by the fishing communities of City Island in the Bronx and Sheepshead Bay in Brooklyn. In "Little Odessa By the Sea" in Brighton Beach, Russian Jews have settled and decorated the landscape with icons of their culture and cuisine. And scores of neighborhoods throughout the boroughs offer a taste of internationalism: the Hispanic cultures in Jackson Heights and the Greek settlement in Astoria, Queens; the small Italian enclave of Arthur Avenue in the Bronx; and the Middle Easterners on Atlantic Avenue in Brooklyn, to name a few. Adventuresome, intellectually curious walking-tour guides love to lead groups to these neighborhoods.

Of all the outer-borough neighborhoods, Brooklyn Heights holds the most allure for tour-takers. It's conveniently close to Manhattan, and, at the same time, sufficiently remote to have retained its architectural charm and authenticity. More than half of its buildings went up before 1860, and they have undergone fewer alterations than Manhattan's buildings from a comparable period.

Brooklyn Heights began as a small Dutch outpost of Manhattan. A sail ferry operated between Manhattan and Brooklyn (originally *Breukelen,* named for a Dutch town outside of Amsterdam and anglicized to *Brooklyn* by the British). In 1814, Robert Fulton's steam ferry, the Nassau, turned Brooklyn into a booming community. By 1834 it became incorporated as a city, easily accessible from Manhattan by several ferries.

In 1883 the Brooklyn Bridge tied the destinies of Manhattan and Brooklyn closer together. Elevated trains used the bridge by the end of the nineteenth century. And in 1908 the first of the subway tunnels leading to Brooklyn went into operation. Oddly enough, though it was easy to travel between Brooklyn Heights and Manhattan, the Heights has remained a relatively unspoiled "bedroom suburb." The residents preserved its fine architecture and noncommercial character. Indeed, in 1965 Brooklyn Heights was the first New York City community to receive landmark status as a historic district. Now, by law, it's impossible to change its quaint appearance.

This chapter gives sketches of the Heights and other tour destinations in the boroughs. Some guides can design tours on request to neighborhoods for which there are few or no existing tours. Tours in the boroughs began after renowned guide Barry Lewis called attention to valuable architecture in Jackson Heights, Queens. The publicity surrounding his walks, originally sponsored by the Queens Historical Society and the Municipal Art Society, actually caused real-estate prices to rise. Historical societies of the boroughs schedule walks every year to their prime neighborhoods. And neighborhood associations also lead occasional tours, usually to visit houses opened to the public for an annual occasion.

Brooklyn

Adventure on a Shoestring, led by its founder, Howard Goldberg, crosses the Brooklyn Bridge on foot annually on May 24, the anniversary of the bridge's opening.

"Wild Man" Steve Brill leads his wild-food walks in Prospect and Marine parks, from mid-March to mid-December. In Brooklyn, walks usually take place twice a month.

The **Brooklyn Botanic Gardens** schedules weekend walks, from spring through mid-November, to see seasonal flowers, free of charge. The gardens are located at 1000 Washington Avenue, 718–622–4433.

The **Brooklyn Heights Association** has sponsored a tour of houses, including an 1834 Federal-style house whose exterior was used as Cher's home in the movie *Moonstruck.* Call 718–858–9193.

The **Brooklyn Historical Society** schedules neighborhood tours between March and November, some geared to school children, others to adults, for small fees. In July and August tours go to Brighton Beach, Fort Hamilton, and Sheepshead Bay on Saturdays and Sundays. In September the destinations are Fulton Ferry Landing, the historic landing for the first steamers, Clinton Hill, Flatbush, and Bay Ridge. Among the leaders for the society are Justin Ferate, John Kriskiewicz, who leads

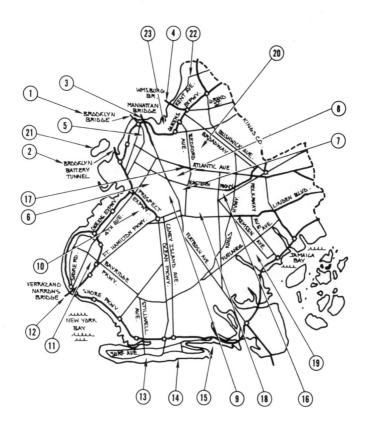

Points of Interest in Brooklyn

1. Brooklyn Bridge
2. Brooklyn Battery Tunnel
3. Manhattan Bridge
4. Williamsburg Bridge
5. Brooklyn Heights/Borough Hall/Promenade/Historical Society
6. Park Slope
7. Prospect Park and Grand Army Plaza
8. Brooklyn Museum
9. Brooklyn Botanic Garden
10. Greenwood Cemetery
11. Bay Ridge Section
12. Verrazano Narrows Bridge
13. Coney Island Section/New York Aquarium
14. Brighton Beach
15. Sheepshead Bay section
16. Crown Heights
17. Atlantic Avenue
18. Flatbush
19. Canarsie
20. Bedford Stuyvesant section
21. Governor's Island
22. Greenpoint
23. Fort Greene

tours in Brooklyn only, and Columbia University professor Andrew Dolkart.

Doorway to Design schedules tours to Brooklyn Heights that concentrate on the neighborhood's varied nineteenth-century architecture, with a walk on the Promenade. From that vantage point, one sees the historic seaport of Manhattan with special clarity. The firm also visits Park Slope, a neighborhood with a vast array of brownstones; the group usually visits one private home. The firm's guides have backgrounds as museum professionals, historians, writers, designers, or architects.

Justin Ferate, a Brooklyn specialist, has led many tours of Brooklyn Heights. For an idea of his route in the Heights, read the description (see p. 192) of the tour offered by the New-York Historical Society, which covers the highlights of most guides.

Ferate, a full-time guide who works for major institutions, historical societies, library associations, and out-of-town tour groups, emphasizes history, architecture, and education. He likes to lead tours of the countrylike mansions of Flatbush, the fishing community of Sheepshead Bay, the Russian community by the elevated train in Brighton Beach, and Coney Island with its historic boardwalk section, amusements, and "a real side show," as Ferate calls it. He goes to Park Slope for its nineteenth-century architecture; he also likes the nineteenth-century row houses in the area of Bedford Stuyvesant known as Stuyvesant Heights, with its glorious homes.

He also goes to the Brooklyn Botanic Gardens, to the Brooklyn Museum, especially for its Egyptian and American paintings collections; to Bay Ridge, an Italian-Irish-Greek-Chinese neighborhood high above the Verrazano Narrows Bridge, with the feeling, in Ferate's estimation, of a small town in the Midwest; to Prospect Park, designed by Olmsted and Vaux, the architects of Central Park (who did a better job, some believe, with the Brooklyn park); and Clinton Hill, for a look at the home of Charles Pratt, a secret partner of John D. Rockefeller, Sr., before the break-up of Standard Oil.

Fort Greene Landmarks Preservation Committee, P.O. Box

401198, Brooklyn, NY 11240-1198; 718–237–9031, occasionally organizes tours of the neighborhood's nineteenth-century houses. The small
fees for the tour go for the preservation of landmarks. One of them is
the house of Samuel Booth, the last mayor of Brooklyn before it became
incorporated into the city of New York.

Marvin Gelfand's Walk of the Town leads tours to several Brooklyn
neighborhoods, including Brooklyn Heights and the Jewish section of
Williamsburg, where he grew up. He starts at the Williamsburg Savings
Bank, referred to as "The Temple" because of the architectural style of
this 1875 landmark building. From there he proceeds to some great
mansions built on Bedford Avenue in the 1890s, now used mostly as
yeshivas. In their heyday, the mansions were residences of such people
as the president of Metropolitan Life, brewers, sugar refiners, and several wealthy Jewish businessmen. In the neighborhood, too, the tour
group views blocks of row houses as interesting in design—and virtually
as hidden from the mainstream—as row houses in Park Slope and
Harlem.

At Bridge Plaza, Gelfand points out a statue of George Washington
depicted at Valley Forge. Another well-known landmark in the community is Peter Luger's Steak House, at 178 Broadway, which Alfred
Hitchcock is reputed to have loved. Henry Miller grew up in the neighborhood. So did novelist Chaim Potok, author of *The Chosen;* a film
made from his novel used Williamsburg's branch of the public library as
a setting. To end the tour, Gelfand leads people across the Williamsburg
Bridge, giving them an aerial view of the commercial character of the
area, and arrives in Manhattan at Delancey Street.

Michael George in Brooklyn Heights talks about the development of
Brooklyn as the country's fourth largest city and stresses the history and
style of the buildings and the political, economic, social, and religious
forces that shaped the Heights.

Val Ginter's Ginter-Gotham Urban History tours Brooklyn Heights
and the Fulton Ferry district. He begins at Brooklyn Borough Hall, built
between 1836 and 1849, and Cadman Plaza, built in the 1950s and

among the first sights one sees after crossing the Brooklyn Bridge into the Heights. He points out the historic sights along Joralemon, Montague, and Pierrepont streets, with their impressive mansions and churches, and heads for the Promenade, built in 1951, continuing from that bucolic riverside viewpoint to some of the fine, surviving examples of mid-1830s architecture along Orange, Pineapple, and Cranberry streets—called the "fruit streets"—and the 1820 building, Brooklyn Heights's oldest, at 24 Middagh Street.

Beginning in 1642 rowboats ferried people from Peck Slip in New Amsterdam (the South Street Seaport area today) to a landing at the western end of Ferry Road in Breukelen. Washington's Army escaped from there in 1776, after losing the Battle of Long Island. In 1814 Robert Fulton inaugurated the steam ferry service between Fulton Street in Manhattan and Fulton Street in Brooklyn.

Along the way, Ginter makes sure to discourse on some of the most important sights in the neighborhood: the Brooklyn Bridge; the former Brooklyn City Railroad Company Building, dating back to 1861 and converted to cooperatives in 1975; the River Café; the urban renewal project of Cadman Towers; Plymouth Church of the Pilgrims, dating back to 1847 and run by the influential abolitionist, Congregationalist minister Henry Ward Beecher, from its inception to 1887; the Hotel St. George; the Diocesan Church of St. Ann and the Holy Trinity; the neo-Romanesque Manufacturers Hanover Trust bank branch built in 1915; St. Francis College Library; the Appellate Division of New York State Supreme Court building on the northwest corner of Monroe and Pierrepoint streets; and the Long Island Historical Society at the southwest corner of Clinton and Pierrepont streets—almost all buildings from the nineteenth century.

To end the tour, Ginter heads back to Borough Hall via Remsen Street. In the Heights, walkers cannot fail to notice the pretty little Greenwich Village-style enclave of restaurants and boutiques, in a quiet atmosphere far more bucolic than Manhattan's. Miraculously, despite its closeness to Manhattan, the Heights has suffered none of the blight of many Queens and Bronx neighborhoods similarly close to the Big Apple. And the tour underscores the lingering suburban character of the Heights.

Brooklyn

Jeffrey Kroessler, a specialist in Queens and Brooklyn, leads tours in Greenpoint, Brighton Beach, Coney Island, and Atlantic Avenue in Brooklyn, from a historical and social point of view.

In Greenpoint, he looks at how the nineteenth-century waterfront has been adapted for use in the twentieth century. There are remnants of abandoned parks, empty houses, and vacant lots here, as well as a Polish-Catholic community.

For his Brighton Beach tour, he starts in Sheepshead Bay and goes to Lundy's, which was an old, well-known seafood restaurant but is now empty. Crossing the bay, with its fleet of fishing boats, he heads for the boardwalk, talking about hotels that were built there, and continues to neighboring Brighton Beach, now a predominantly Russian community. Any tour visiting on a Sunday will be likely to see spectacularly festive parties in the restaurants, as the Russians celebrate family occasions; the vodka flows like wine, and the caviar is set out as lavishly as if it were chopped liver. Kroessler looks at Brighton Beach's art deco buildings put up in the 1930s and also at the Brighton Beach baths.

He leads a separate tour of Coney Island. Along the boardwalk, he shows people the amusement-park rides and talks about their history. He visits the Steeplechase, an amusement park built in 1910, torn down in the 1960s, and now a vacant lot. The tour also features Nathan's hotdogs, which are still alive and well in the Nathan's Famous shop started as a boardwalk bargain by Nathan Handwerker, a German Jewish immigrant. The New York Aquarium is located in Coney Island, too, a fascinating, well-stocked preserve for those interested in marine life; it has provided a home for everything from bright blue lobsters the color of Paul Newman's eyes to spearlike sharks.

Kroessler's Atlantic Avenue tour begins at the Long Island Railroad Station in Brooklyn, proceeds to Atlantic Avenue to view the Lebanese community's restaurants and stores, and goes on to the nineteenth-century Brooklyn neighborhood, Cobble Hill, where many buildings have been upgraded recently for residences. Kroessler stresses the proximity of nineteenth-century American row houses to twentieth-century immigrant ethnic neighborhoods—a blend of cultures that lends a special flavor to Brooklyn.

Brooklyn

Barry Lewis teaches "Neighborhoods in Transition," a course under the aegis of the Municipal Art Society about the outer boroughs. He feels that Manhattan has been overexposed; in the outer boroughs, one can find lovely neighborhoods, which he thinks have been overlooked. Lewis takes tours to Flatbush and other Brooklyn neighborhoods, emphasizing current developments as well as new and recycled buildings, condominiums, and streets. An archaeological and urban historian, he says that he's "as interested in the mean streets as I am in the architecture." He covers all the boroughs in his course. In Brooklyn, he visits downtown Brooklyn, Clinton Hill, Bedford Stuyvesant, Crown Heights, Flatbush, Sunset Park, Bay Ridge, and Brooklyn Heights. Aware that parts of certain neighborhoods have developed such intimidating reputations that people think they'll be murdered while on a walking tour, he has discovered: "People can be fascinated, without any feeling of danger."

The Municipal Art Society, in addition to Barry Lewis's course on "Neighborhoods in Transition," which goes to all the boroughs, has scheduled walks focusing on Brooklyn's immigrant neighborhoods; Brooklyn Heights, including the Promenade, Greenpoint, and Flatbush, for a nostalgic view of once-grand movie theaters. As usual, the M.A.S. tour destinations vary widely from year to year, depending on the areas of current concern to the society regarding the quality of life in New York City.

The **Museum of the City of New York,** in addition to its Walt Whitman days tour from Soho to Brooklyn Heights, outlined in chapter 4, leads a tour totally within the confines of Brooklyn Heights. The walk begins at the statue of Beecher near the back steps of Borough Hall, proceeds to 1 Pierrepont Plaza, the newest and tallest skyscraper in Brooklyn, and then to the elegant Montague Street branch of Manufacturers Hanover Trust, which went up before the Depression, when other banks were failing. The branch has delightful architectural details, down to its bronze desks for customers. The group also passes by the Diocesan Church of St. Ann and the Holy Trinity and the First Unitarian Church, both Gothic Revival designs by Minard Lafever, a well-known architect of his period, and the Brooklyn Historical Society, which recently had a name change from the Long Island Historical Society, on the way to the Height's Promenade. The tour then heads to the Plymouth Church of the Pilgrims, Beecher's church.

The museum also schedules a tour of historic Park Slope, a residential neighborhood noted for its classic Victorian Era brownstones. The Park Slope district ranges from the west of Flatbush Avenue, Plaza Street, and Prospect Park West to the east of an imaginary line starting at Sixth Avenue and Flatbush Avenue, and runs south, cutting a zigzag swath through the grid streets, to Bartel-Pritchard Square.

Within this area, Litchfield Villa was built in 1857 by architect Alexander Jackson Davis for Edwin C. Litchfield. The latter made a fortune in midwestern railroad development, then acquired most of the empty land that would one day be called Park Slope. His Italianate mansion now serves as the Brooklyn Parks Department headquarters on Prospect Park West between Fourth and Fifth streets. The original stucco exterior has been scraped to expose the brick underneath.

Prospect Park itself, designed by Frederick Law Olmsted and Calvert Vaux, took shape between 1866 and 1874. By the 1880s, the adjacent Park Slope area began to see the residences that inspired people to nickname Plaza Street and Prospect Park West the "Gold Coast." This lavish collection of Victorian mansions and row houses in brick and brownstone dominated the area until after World War I. Then massive apartment buildings went up around Grand Army Plaza at the intersection of Flatbush Avenue, Prospect Park West, Eastern Parkway, and Vanderbilt Avenue. The apartments substantially completed Park Slope's development.

Olmsted and Vaux modeled Grand Army Plaza on L'Etoile in Paris. John H. Duncan's Soldiers' and Sailors' Memorial Arch, dedicated to the Union forces in the Civil War, was erected more than two decades later, in 1892. In 1895 two bas reliefs inside the arch, one of Lincoln by Thomas Eakins, the other of Grant by William O'Donovan, were installed. In 1898 Frederick MacMonnies's giant quadriga—a chariot drawn by four horses abreast—went on top, and in 1901 MacMonnies's groups The Army and The Navy took their places on the south pedestals.

Brooklyn

To the north of the arch on another traffic island stands the 1965 John F. Kennedy Memorial, by Morris Ketchum, Jr., & Associates, architects, and Neil Estern, sculptor; and the Bailey Fountain, Edgerton Swarthwout, architect, and Eugene Savage, sculptor, with its bronze mass of tritons and Neptune.

The New-York Historical Society's tour of Brooklyn was so popular in 1988 that the crowd was broken up into several groups. One was led by Justin Ferate; another by the director of the walking-tour program for the society, Arthur Marks; another by Jeff Sholeen; and more sections by a handful of other veteran New York City guides. All sections of the tour followed approximately the same route, and the leaders emphasized the treasure trove of architecture here.

This tour begins at Borough Hall, where the guides scrutinize a statue of Henry Ward Beecher (1818–1887), the brother of Harriet Beecher Stowe, who wrote the highly successful, melodramatic *Uncle Tom's Cabin.* Henry Beecher was a renowned Congregationalist preacher in Brooklyn Heights, to which he migrated from New England. Well loved by his parishioners, he was a staunch Abolitionist. Brooklyn was an excellent place for him to air his views, because, according to some guides, Manhattan, wrapped up in the economics of its cotton warehouses on Chambers Street, nearly seceded with the South during the Civil War. From New York, the cotton was shipped to England. But Brooklyn was farmland with a self-contained community and an economy independent of Southern-grown cotton. Brooklynites would not be economically affected by an Abolitionist position. And Beecher's antislavery position was very popular.

Some guides discourse at length about Brooklyn's position during the Revolutionary War and the War of 1812, when the waterfront had many forts. Then groups cross Cadman Plaza to view some notable buildings. One is the former National Title Guaranty building at 185 Montague Street, described as a German Expressionist or art deco building. Another interesting, very pretty building is a Florentine palace—a branch of Manufacturers Hanover Trust, with a multicolored mosaic floor as one of its stunning features.

Guides explain how Brooklyn Heights residents rallied to get the neighborhood declared a historic district, after they were appalled by the demolition of the old Pennsylvania Station: built to last more than 1,000 years, it was torn down after only fifty-four. But it was, in a sense, a sacrifice that led to laws against the possibility of a similar tragedy in Brooklyn Heights.

The tour also visits the Diocesan Church of St. Ann and the Holy Trinity on Clinton and Montague streets. Built in 1847, it was originally called the Holy Trinity Church. In those days, it had a steeple, but that was removed when the BMT subway was built: the vibrations made it likely that the steeple would fall one day and injure people. An exuberantly Gothic church of brownstone and limestone with an exterior of variegated colors and textures, this national and city landmark is disintegrating because of the inferior quality of the brownstone.

The tour proceeds along Pierrepont Street. No. 104 Pierrepont, done in an 1850s Italianate style, is a good example of a typical row house—four stories high, twenty-two feet wide. The tour wends its way along Pierrepont to the Promenade. Along the way, anecdotes about the life-styles of the rather sedate original settlers of Brooklyn Heights—Calvinists, Congregationalists, and Unitarians—come up. One clipper-ship owner's idea of fun, for example, was to situate his house near the water, so that he could keep an eye on his boats going to and coming from China. However, one does sense a trace of sex appeal in the shape of an 1891 Romanesque Revival-style house on Pierrepont Street, which was once a hotel popular with prostitutes; later it was taken over by the Franciscan Brothers; now it's a cooperative apartment house. Another hint of sex appeal comes from tales of Henry Ward Beecher's dalliances with women in his congregation. He was an attractive, mesmerizing figure and so well loved in the community that the scandals surrounding his personal life never threatened his professional position.

From Pierrepont, with a foray onto the Promenade, groups head along Willow Street, to Pineapple, Orange, Cranberry and Middagh streets, usually finishing their walks in front of the Plymouth Church of the Pilgrims, Beecher's church, a quaint, plain brick box. Beecher preached in Brooklyn from 1847 to 1887; the church was completed in 1849.

Brooklyn

New York Walkabout has a tour of Brooklyn Heights called "Forgotten by Time" that focuses on the remarkably preserved nineteenth-century community of historic buildings. They predate, for the most part, the Civil War and to this day provide one of the pleasantest residential spots in New York City.

The **92nd Street "Y"** has several tours of special interest to the Jewish community. One is a "Borough Park Pre-Passover Tour," which has been led in the past by a rabbi who lives in this Orthodox Jewish neighborhood. The tour visits a matzo factory, houses of worship, and a mikvah. Men are advised to have head covers, or yarmulkas, handy, and women should wear modest dresses or skirts. "Jewish Williamsburg" is another "Y"-sponsored tour, also led by a resident of the community. On this tour you will visit the Satmars, a secluded Hasidic group, see their religious sites, and observe their street life, which seems to have survived from an earlier century in Eastern Europe.

Justin Ferate has led the usual tour of Brooklyn Heights for the "Y." He and another Brooklyn expert, John Kriskiewicz, have led tours of Coney Island, visiting the Boardwalk, the historic sights, recounting its development and ending with lunch at Nathan's Famous. The "Y" has also sponsored the novelty tour of a walk across the Brooklyn Bridge to Fulton Ferry Landing to examine the development of the area, including its restaurants, and to attend a concert aboard "Bargemusic," a floating concert hall. This tour has been scheduled, in the past, to take place on Mother's Day.

The "Y" sponsors a tour entitled "Seagate: A Private Community." Seagate was originally a sailing community founded in 1899 on Norton Point, facing the Atlantic Ocean and the Lower Bay at the western tip of Coney Island. Once an expensive and exclusive Anglo-American summer resort, Seagate now has a considerable number of representatives of numerous ethnic groups, especially Italians, Greeks, and Hasidic Jews. It is a private community of forty-three square blocks and about 900 pretty little houses, approached through a guarded gate. The Coney Island boardwalk goes close enough to allow sightseers a view from the outside. The group has a picnic lunch in Lindbergh Park.

Other Brooklyn tours under the aegis of the "Y" go to Brighton Beach's Russian Jewish community, Flatbush's turn-of-the-century mansions, and the fifty-acre Brooklyn Botanic Gardens, with its herb, rose, rock, and tranquil Japanese meditation gardens, and a noted Bonsai collection.

In its "Behind the Scenes" series, the "Y" has organized outings to the Brooklyn Academy of Music for a performance plus a visit backstage with the cast.

Since "Y" tours are scheduled on an irregular basis and not every tour takes place each year, call the "Y" for its current plans.

Everett Ortner, a resident in a Park Slope brownstone and chairman of the Brownstone Revival Committee of New York, founded in 1968, leads tours of Park Slope and Brooklyn Heights to explore their caches of brownstones. His wife, also a brownstone aficionado, with a graduate degree in architectural preservation from Columbia University, assists him.

Sometimes tours begin by bus, usually near the Waldorf-Astoria Hotel, visit several brownstone sites in Manhattan on the Upper West Side and Greenwich Village, then cross to Brooklyn's nineteenth-century communities. Fort Greene and Bedford-Stuyvesant are occasionally added to the itinerary. The group ends with lunch at the Montauk Club, a 100-year-old Venetian Gothic landmark building in Park Slope.

The **Park Rangers** lead a variety of walks in Prospect Park by day to see the butterflies, beginning at the park entrance at 16th Street and Prospect Park Southwest; to examine bee communities and reptiles, on two different walks, both beginning at the Prospect Park boathouse, reached by the park entrance at Ocean Avenue and Lincoln Road; to visit the zoo, from the Willink entrance, Empire Boulevard and Flatbush Avenue; to see the birds or study the stars, on walks beginning at Grand Army Plaza; to visit a Quaker Cemetery within the park, in which actor Montgomery Clift is buried; or to learn compass and map skills on walks beginning at Prospect Park West and Third Street. Occasionally the Rangers organize horseback rides through the park. You must call for the schedule.

Brooklyn

In Manhattan Beach, beginning at Oriental Boulevard and Hastings Street, the Rangers lead walks to see marine life. At Marine Park, beginning in the Avenue U parking lot, between E. 33rd and Burnett streets, the Rangers lead walks to see wildflowers, birds, and other wildlife.

The Rangers also lead occasional tours for wildlife and history in Owls Head Park at 68th Street and Colonial Road, and in Fort Greene Park, starting from the Visitors Center near the Prison Ship Martyr's Monument, reached from the entrance at St. Edwards Street and Myrtle Avenue. Again, be sure to call the Park Rangers for the schedule.

The **Prospect Park Environmental Center,** c/o The Tennis House in Prospect Park, leads tours year-round on weekends, focusing on urban architecture and history. The center's director is urban geographer John Muir, a former professor at City University of New York. Some tours are geared to children, others to adults. About half the tours take place in Prospect Park; the rest are usually in Brooklyn. Subjects have ranged from a Halloween tour to a historic cemetery to do gravestone rubbings, to a walk through Coney Island's subway yards, to a railroad tunnel under Atlantic Avenue, to constructions sites.

Joseph L. Schiff, the head of Jewish Urban Study Tours, seeks to educate people in the history of the Jews in New York City by looking for traces of the community in the streets. He offers several tours in Brooklyn, including "The World of Hasidism and Halacha" in Borough Park, in the course of which he raises (and answers) such questions as: "What is Jewish law?" "What is the infrastructure of a Hasidic community?" In Borough Park he finds about twenty different Hasidic groups to illustrate his lectures. He takes other tours to Crown Heights for another aspect of Hasidism.

Professor James Shenton, from Columbia University's history department, counts Brighton Beach, Brooklyn Heights, and the Brooklyn Bridge among his favorite walking tours. He leads the Brighton Beach tour rarely, because it takes about eighty minutes to reach this neighborhood from midtown Manhattan. If you can't find a tour going there, Shenton recommends that you take yourself to see the Russian Jewish community life, the restaurants, and the shops. Dr. Shenton has observed that the community is actually a Russian one, which happens to be Jewish: the customs are 100 percent Russian. Contemporary American Jews do not set out bottles of vodka on the table as if they were wine and drink the potent stuff without any ice. And in general, in their social relationships, within families and with friends, the Russians form a distinct community, which they regard as a safe harbor in an unfamiliar land.

Dr. Shenton combines Brooklyn Heights with the Brooklyn Bridge for a tour. Crossing the bridge, he believes, gives sightseers a sense of the dimensions of the harbor and an understanding of poet Hart Crane's ode to the bridge. In Dr. Shenton's view, which he shares with others, Brooklyn Heights is New York's answer to Boston's Beacon Hill. He goes all the way to Atlantic Avenue, the Middle Eastern enclave at the southern border of Brooklyn Heights.

Jeff Sholeen, who leads tours in Manhattan and Brooklyn, with notable expertise in the Victorian and modern periods, likes to tour Brooklyn Heights. He begins at Borough Hall, a Greek Revival building erected between 1836 and 1849, on the site where Brooklyn's old business section used to be. From Cadman Plaza, which faces Borough Hall, he walks north to the statue of Henry Ward Beecher, the famed nineteenth-century Congregationalist minister, and then crosses Court Street, heading toward the upper harbor.

Sometimes he opts to take a Remsen Street route. There he shows the old headquarters of Brooklyn Union Gas Co., which was called the Brooklyn Gas Light Co. when it occupied the 1857 building that is the library at St. Francis College. Then he continues to the southeast corner of Clinton and Remsen, where cooperative apartments now exist inside a former Presbyterian church.

If, instead, he takes Montague Street, a main commercial artery in Brooklyn Heights, he highlights a group of interesting buildings—the predecessors of the Brooklyn Library, the Brooklyn Academy of Music, and the Brooklyn Museum; all once had their headquarters on the block between Court and Clinton streets, along Montague Street. Passing a 1915 branch of Manufacturers Hanover Trust Co., he comes to an 1847 church by Minard Lefever—the Diocesan Church of St. Ann and the Holy Trinity—an example of Gothic Revival design, with very famous, early American-made stained-glass windows currently being restored.

Then he walks along Pierrepont Street, where the Brooklyn Historical Society was built in 1878 in a Romanesque Revival/eclectic style. Its architect, George B. Post, also designed the New York Stock Exchange. Going east along Pierrepont toward the river, Sholeen points out many important mansions, some of which were built as private homes. At 55 Pierrepont, the Horace Claflin mansion has become an apartment building. In the 1860s Claflin was a wealthy wholesaler from New England. It's possible that a daughter of Claflin's was romantically entangled with Henry Ward Beecher, who reportedly had numerous affairs with members of his congregation.

Sholeen continues along Pierrepont, to Pierrepont Place just behind the Promenade, formally named the Esplanade, from which there is a wonderful view of Manhattan's harbor and skyline. A couple of mid-nineteenth-century houses still stand there, among them No. 2, an 1857 brownstone mansion; missing is No. 1, which was the house of Henry E. Pierrepont, son of Hezekiah Pierrepont, a prominent Brooklyn Heights landowner.

The group then walks north along Willow Street, passing 1830 Greek Revival houses, an 1820s Federal-style house, and a carriage house in which Arthur Miller was reported to have lived before he married Marilyn Monroe. Further north, on Willow Street, stand more Federalist buildings of wood, brick, and stucco. Several streets in this area are named for fruits: Orange, Pineapple, and Cranberry. North of the "fruit streets," Henry Ward Beecher lived in an 1846 Greek Revival house, at 22 Willow Street, near Middagh, which had a huge back porch to take advantage of the breezes off the river. At 24 Middagh Street stands a wooden house with a gambrel roof built in 1820; the roof slopes twice, as a barn's roof does. This house is believed to be the oldest still standing in Brooklyn Heights. From there, the tour continues to the Plymouth Church of the Pilgrims, which was simply called Plymouth Church when Henry Ward Beecher was its Congregational minister. The tour ends here.

Occasionally, for tours that request an extra fillip, Sholeen adds a walk to the Riverside Buildings, 4–30 Columbia Place, in the southwest corner of Brooklyn Heights. Some of these houses, put up as a bid at philanthropy with a 5 percent profit for the owners, were torn down to make way for the Brooklyn-Queens Expressway. But a portion of these brick and iron buildings with balconies still stands. Another, similar project in Cobble Hill remains intact.

Sholeen occasionally adds another church to his tour. Now called Our Lady of Lebanon Maronite Catholic Cathedral on Remsen Street, it was formerly the Church of the Pilgrims, a Congregational church, in the nineteenth century. At that time, many Congregationalists moved from New England to Brooklyn Heights and established themselves as a hard-working, church-going merchant class, with Abolitionist sympathies. Richard Upjohn, architect for Trinity Church in Lower Manhattan's historic district, designed this church, too. It now has the added attraction of art deco doors, which were taken from the Normandie, a ship that burned and sank in its Hudson River berth.

Lou Singer's tours of the Lower East Side and the best places to go "noshing," or snacking, in New York, have been written about in the *New Yorker*'s "Talk of the Town" section. He also has expertise as a Brooklyn guide. His repertoire includes:

- Brownstone neighborhoods in Brooklyn Heights, Cobble Hill, Carroll Gardens, Park Slope, Clinton, and Fort Greene, with visits to private houses and a church with Tiffany windows
- Brooklyn Heights and Cobble Hill combined
- Park Slope, including Prospect Park's Litchfield Villa
- Clinton and Fort Greene, running the gamut from a Presbyterian church with eighteen Tiffany windows to a Satmar Hasidic community
- Flatbush, including a 1654 Dutch Reformed Church and the first film studios in the United States
- Brooklyn's waterfront, including Coney Island, Sea Gate, Bay Ridge, Sunset Park, Brighton Beach, and Sheepshead Bay

199

• Brooklyn's ethnic communities—Polish, Russian, Hasidic, German, Black, Scandinavian, and Italian, in the neighborhoods of Greenpoint, Williamsburg, Ridgewood, Bedford-Stuyvesant, Bay Ridge, Bensonhurst, and Brighton Beach.

Singer also leads tours for special-interest groups—to see churches, or Russian nightclubs, or the Christmas lights of Bensonhurst and Canarsie, for example.

Joe Zito, whose specialty is Hell's Kitchen in Manhattan, lived in Flatbush for forty years and leads tours all around Brooklyn as well as Manhattan. In Brooklyn, he has led tours for the Brooklyn Historical Society and Long Island University's Department of Urban Affairs. He has given many tours of Brooklyn Heights, beginning at the Historical Society.

The Bronx

"Wild Man" Steve Brill, rotating joyously between the parks for his forays for wild plants, flowers, fruits, mushrooms, herbs, nuts, seeds and roots, leads walks in the Bronx River Park, Pelham Bay Park, and Van Cortlandt Park as part of his schedule under the auspices of the New York Department of Parks and Recreation.

The **Bronx Historical Society,** which boasts that the Bronx is the only borough that is actually a part of the mainland, was founded in 1955 to preserve and promote the heritage of this large metropolitan area. The borough has a Museum of Bronx History located in the Valentine-Varian House, a fieldstone farmhouse built in 1758. The Edgar Allan Poe Cottage, built in 1812, is preserved as a memorial. The Historical Society also has a library and publishes a semiannual journal about the Bronx's history. The society will organize walking tours for private groups on request. As part of a regular program, walking tours take place in warm weather.

Some tours cross the Bronx. Others go into the borough's parks or along the Bronx Heritage Trail or to the Great Salt Marsh of Co-op City.

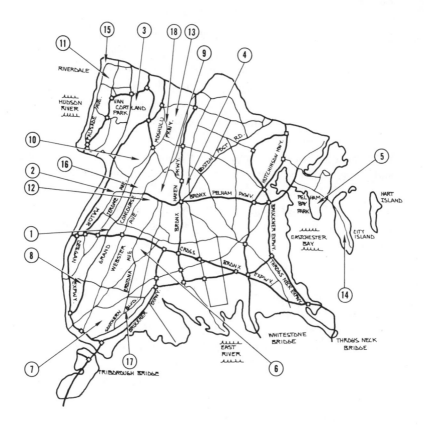

Points of Interest in the Bronx

1. Grand Concourse
2. Fordham Road
3. Van Cortlandt Park
4. Bronx Park
5. Pelham Bay Park
6. Crotona Park
7. Mott Haven and the South Bronx
8. Yankee Stadium
9. Fordham University
10. Herbert H. Lehman College
11. Riverdale
12. Arthur Avenue
13. Woodlawn Cemetery
14. City Island
15. Wave Hill Environmental Center
16. Poe Cottage
17. Longwood Historic District
18. Moshulu Parkway

The Bronx

Tours visit the South Bronx and Bedford Park for their art deco architecture. There's a tour of country clubs and also the Belmont area of the Bronx, including Arthur Avenue, the Italian section. Walks go to Fordham Road, Yankee Village, City Island, Woodlawn Cemetery, the elegant community of Riverdale, and various colleges and universities including, of course, Fordham University.

Val Ginter's Ginter-Gotham Urban History visits both Mott Haven and Longwood. The central street of the Mott Haven Historic District, bounded by E. 137th and E. 141st streets, Third Avenue and Willis Avenue, is Alexander Avenue. Ginter calls it "the old Irish Fifth Avenue." This tour of the South Bronx includes many examples of fine old architecture.

Barry Lewis, who feels at home in every borough, schedules tours to the South Bronx, from Mott Haven to the Hub to Morrisania, and then heads for lunch to Arthur Avenue in the enduring Italian neighborhood of Belmont. A small enclave, this neighborhood has more authenticity than Little Italy in Manhattan from the historian's point of view, because tourists don't visit Arthur Avenue so readily or easily. And Arthur Avenue's community both lives and works in the neighborhood. Lewis also leads a walking tour of Fordham Road, the Grand Concourse—once an elegant residential area and now the Bronx's downtown—and Parkchester, a suburban-style enclave with many cooperatives.

The **Municipal Art Society** is currently sponsoring a lecture/walking-tours course, "Neighborhoods in Transition," taught by Barry Lewis; he schedules his Bronx tours for the course, as well as for other groups.

The **Park Rangers** have programs of tours for schoolchildren in Crotona, Pelham Bay, and Van Cortlandt parks. In Crotona Park's 147 acres, kids are taught about animals and how they adapt to their environment; e.g., squirrels have claws for tree climbing, and butterflies have long tongues for collecting nectar. And there are snails, snapping turtles, and diving beetles in the pond.

Pelham Bay Park occupies 2,764 acres in the northeast section of the Bronx, with salt marshes, forests, meadows, and numerous geological formations. Students are taken to the Pelham Bay Environmental Center located at Section Two of Orchard Beach, and, after a half-hour lecture, they're escorted to a waterfront or a forest, to learn about the plant and animal life and the interrelationships of the ecological systems. In Van Cortlandt Park, all tours begin at the Visitors Center at 242nd Street and Broadway, and the tours encompass plants, trees, urban animals—raccoons, herons, bees, frogs, and others—and many of the nature lessons taught in Crotona Park, too.

Professor James Shenton, of Columbia University's department of history, occasionally visits Arthur Avenue, even though it is one of his favorite tour destinations because of its vital, compact, dynamic culture. The train ride to the Italian enclave in the Bronx is long (if you get off at Fordham Road and walk to Arthur Avenue) and the area is remote, but once you arrive, you find a self-contained, authentic neighborhood. Many of the businessmen and restaurateurs in Little Italy, in Manhattan, travel to work from their homes in Brooklyn and New Jersey, to perpetuate a facsimile of a once-thriving neighborhood. And they sustain the neighborhood primarily as a tourist attraction. But Arthur Avenue's working-class population has no pretense; it lives and works in the same place. And the restaurant cuisine is genuinely homespun, with homemade ricotta cheese, sausages, breads, pastas, and tomato sauces.

Wave Hill Center for Environmental Studies, 249th Street and Independence Avenue, 549–2055, has regularly scheduled Sunday-afternoon walks in its greenhouse and garden, free of charge, and also conducts woodland walks to see wildflowers and plants of all types, and early-morning bird walks, too, for nominal fees—$2 each in 1988.

Queens
Alley Pond Environmental Center, 288-06 Northern Boulevard, Douglaston, Queens, 718–229–4000, schedules a wetlands walk on Sun-

day afternoons for a small fee—$2 in 1988. The center is made up of thousands of acres of marshlands, with birds, a salt marsh, and all that a marsh's ecology entails—horseshoe crabs, for example, which are actually 200-million-year-old fossils.

"Wild Man" Steve Brill makes trips to Alley Pond Marsh, Alley Pond Woods, Flushing Meadow Park, Kissena Park, Cunningham Park, and Forest Park. Because of the variety of parks in Queens, he leads walks there three or four times a month.

Val Ginter's Ginter-Gotham Urban History goes to the Hunter's Point Historic District, just across the river from Manhattan in Queens, near Jackson Avenue; the small enclave of row houses, essentially made up of parts of two blocks, runs along 45th Avenue bounded by 21st and 23rd streets.

Jeffrey Kroessler, a history teacher for the City University of New York with a special interest in Queens history, also leads tours of Hunter's Point—the historic district and the surrounding neighborhood. He points out major changes taking place in Hunter's Point, including a massive waterfront-development project planned by the Port Authority for Long Island City, the new Citicorp tower, and the two-block historic row-house district, and the site of an old ferry and railroad transportation hub. He then walks to Long Island City's row houses and factories and ends the tour at the Beaux Arts Queens County Courthouse, with its notable copper roof, at Courthouse Square.

In Flushing, which contains a new East Asian community of Koreans, Japanese, and Chinese two blocks away from the Queens Historical Society, he discusses the area's Colonial history back to the 1600s and tries to paint a picture of what these blocks, now filled with Asian lettering, looked like 300 years ago. He also emphasizes the current activity in the area; some nineteenth-century buildings are being torn down and replaced by twelve-story high rises. He walks along the Flushing Freedom Mile, which contains a 1690 Quaker Meeting House, established as a national shrine to religious freedom, and also the 1660s

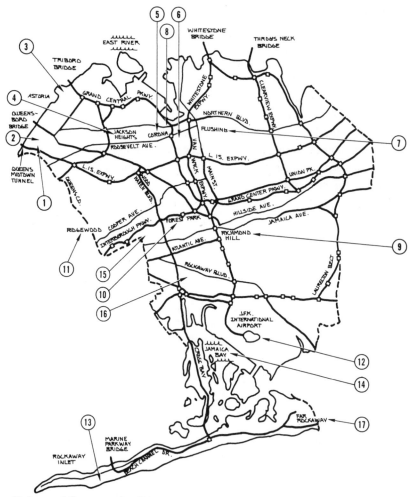

Points of Interest in Queens

1. Hunter's Point Historic District
2. Courthouse Square
3. Astoria
4. Jackson Heights
5. Corona
6. Flushing Meadow Park
7. Flushing
8. Shea Stadium
9. Richmond Hill
10. Forest Park
11. Ridgewood
12. John F. Kennedy International Airport
13. Gateway National Recreation Area
14. Jamaica Bay
15. Highland Park
16. Aqueduct Racetrack
17. Far Rockaway

Queens

Bowne House, which once welcomed Quakers, in opposition to Dutch Governor Peter Stuyvesant's wishes to impose the Dutch Reformed Church on New Netherlands. The Queens Historical Society now occupies a circa 1790s farmhouse, the Kingsland House, one-half block away from the Bowne House and two blocks from the Quaker Meeting House. For another tour of Flushing, he boards the #7 subway train, which leaves Grand Central Station and goes to the end of the line in Flushing. On the trip, he talks about the panorama of Queens as seen from the train. It goes through so many ethnic and historic neighborhoods that Mr. Kroessler in effect feels as if he's talking about different countries. "I don't do this tour during rush hour," he says.

He also leads a tour across the Queensboro Bridge, discussing development on both sides, in Manhattan and Queens, and emphasizing the Queens waterfront.

Barry Lewis, who lives in Queens, as Kroessler does, visits eight neighborhoods for his Queens tours: downtown Jamaica, Richmond Hill, Kew Gardens, Forest Hills, Jackson Heights, Sunnyside Gardens, Long Island City, and Elmhurst, most of them included in his "Neighborhoods in Transition" course currently being taught under the aegis of the Municipal Art Society. He was probably the first person to give tours in Queens. In any case, he was the first to acquire a great deal of publicity and notoriety for doing so.

At one time he led a tour of Jackson Heights for the Municipal Art Society; then the Queens Historical Society, hearing about it, asked him to do a special project on the same neighborhood. He took people along 85th Street between 35th and 34th avenues in Jackson Heights, a neighborhood of semidetached houses that look like small versions of English country mansions, with stables/garages for chauffeurs—"simple but elegant," he sums up. Furthermore, he talked about the neighborhood as a fascinating ethnic melting pot now.

He was often stopped in the street while he was doing his tour and asked: "What is there to see in this neighborhood?" He told people what they were looking at. Eventually, the tour was written up in a newspaper. He has even affected real estate values in Jackson Heights, he has learned. One house was sold not long ago for $375,000 on the block where he leads his tour. Until that sale, no house on the block had ever gone for more than $300,000. The owner proved to the city assessor that the historic value of the house amounted to $375,000, citing the newspaper story and Lewis's notes—and the assessor approved the new valuation.

Richard McDermott, a history and science teacher in Queens and the editor of the *New York Chronicle,* a quarterly journal about historic New York, leads tours in Manhattan primarily; he also leads a natural-history tour in Alley Pond Environmental Center in Douglaston, Queens.

The **Museum of the City of New York** leads a tour called "Latin Imprimaturs: Jackson Heights," which explores a neighborhood that is home to a mélange of immigrants from Latin America—especially from Colombia, Cuba, El Salvador, Peru, and Ecuador. Many of the residents are recent arrivals or first-generation American citizens, and they stay in close touch with the customs and foods of their native cultures. The tour meets at the southeast corner of Roosevelt Avenue and 74th Street in Queens, which can be reached by either the IRT #7 or the IND E and F trains, all of which have a 74th Street stop in Queens. The Museum also introduced a new tour of Flushing's Chinatown, as its Asian community is known, in 1988; the walk is called "Asian Nexus: Flushing."

The 92nd Street "Y" has occasional tours in Queens, such as a trip to the Jamaica Bay Wildlife Refuge, which is filled with water birds. In the sanctuary, which is part of the Federal Gateway National Recreational Area, you learn to identify the birds and understand the environment in which they thrive.

The **Park Rangers** lead tours in Queens for schoolchildren and adults on many topics, ranging from nature to the destructiveness of graffiti in parkland. The majority of walks take place in Kissena Park, but many small parks also have events scheduled. Contact the Park Rangers for information.

Staten Island

The **Queens Historical Society** hires guides to lead neighborhood tours, among the best-known of whom are Jeffrey Kroessler and Barry Lewis. The society offices are open on Tuesdays, Saturdays, and Sundays and feature changing exhibitions shedding light and perspective on Queens history. Kroessler is the curator for the society, Mary Anne Mrozinski the executive director; Kroessler mounts exhibits and gives lectures. Another tour leader for the society is Jack Eichenbaum, an urban geographer, whose repertoire includes the industrial community, College Point, next door to Flushing.

Professor James Shenton, of Columbia University's history department, finds Greek Astoria a lot of fun. For one thing, it's easy to reach: one can take the #7 train from Grand Central Station and change at Queensboro plaza for the N train to Ditmars Boulevard. (or else take the N train directly from Broadway). The neighborhood has the authentic ambience of a small Greek town, with delightful restaurants and shops. When Dr. Shenton leads a tour, he likes to arrange to enter some of the Greek Orthodox churches to round out the visit. On a walk in Astoria with Dr. Shenton, you'll find out about Greek and Cypriot history in Europe, too.

Staten Island
"Wild Man" Steve Brill even gets to 500-acre La Tourette Park for a day of foraging occasionally. His Staten Island tours are so rare, however, that you should call him early in March to find out the schedule. La Tourette Park is at Forest Hill and Richmond Hill roads, in Richmondtown, Staten Island, and is known primarily as a place for golf, horseback riding, and picnics.

Barry Lewis's interests range as far away from the madding crowd of Manhattan to this least citified of the boroughs, where he explores the Victorian rim of Staten Island's northeastern communities—St. George, Stapleton, and New Brighton. You land in St. George when you step off the ferry, and your first impression is definitely of a Victorian landscape.

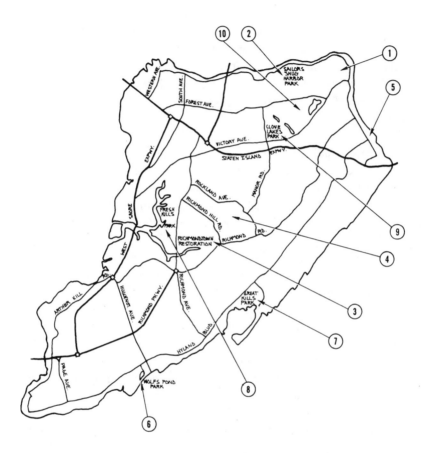

Points of Interest in Staten Island

1. St. George
2. Sailors' Snug Harbor
3. Richmondtown/Staten Island Historical Museum
4. La Tourette Park
5. Jane Austen house
6. Wolf's Pond Park
7. Great Kills Park
8. Fresh Kills Park
9. Clove Lake's Park
10. Silver Lake Park

Staten Island

You feel that you are stepping back 100 years or more in time, with a view of houses that could have served as scenery in Nathaniel Hawthorne's novels and stories. You also find many nineteenth-century buildings in Stapleton and New Brighton. In New Brighton especially, some of the houses are historic landmarks, with a mix of architectural styles popular in the first half of the nineteenth century. One of the oldest houses in New York City, the Neville House, dating back to circa 1770, stands in New Brighton, where it was built by a retired naval officer.

The **Municipal Art Society,** in cooperation with the Prospect Park Environmental Center, sponsored a tour by Barry Lewis in 1988, in connection with his "Neighborhoods in Transition" course for the M.A.S. The tour touched the Victorian rim destinations in Staten Island discussed in the sketch of Lewis, above, and also took in Bay Ridge, Sunset Park, and Flatbush in Brooklyn.

The M.A.S. has also sponsored tours to Sailors' Snug Harbor, at Richmond Terrace, between Tysen Street, Snug Harbor, and Kissel Avenue in Staten Island, built between 1831 and 1880. Once a home for retired sailors, the complex consists of five Greek Revival temples, founded and funded by Robert Richard Randall, the son of a Revolutionary War privateer. The city declared the harbor a landmark in the 1960s; the sailors' home institution moved to the North Carolina coast. Plans also got underway for a $12 million restoration project for the Snug Harbor Cultural Center. In conjunction with that project, the M.A.S. sponsored a tour, including the presence of Rafael Vinoly, the architect who won a competition to restore Snug Harbor's Music Hall. Call the M.A.S. to find out when the Staten Island tours are scheduled.

The M.A.S. has also sponsored restoration-oriented tours to the Statue of Liberty, when the "Lady with the Lamp" was overhauled.

The **Museum of the City of New York** leads a tour group aboard a Staten Island ferry, discussing New York's port, the hard life-style of its seamen, and, in Staten Island, the historic grog shops and fancy houses that attracted the seamen in the harbor in the nineteenth century. Then the group looks at the Greek Revival complex—the five temples of Snug Harbor—first endowed by the son of a Revolutionary War privateer, later governed for years by writer Herman Melville's brother.

New York Walkabout leads a tour of Upper New York Bay and the islands along the ferry route between Manhattan and Staten Island. As you sail along, a guide discusses the history of Governor's Island, Ellis Island, Statue of Liberty Island, and the bay, and Manhattan and Staten Island harbors.

The **92nd Street "Y"** organizes a tour specifically to Governor's Island. The island isn't usually open to the public; it's reached by special ferry, which this tour utilizes. Governor's Island was set aside in 1698 for the "benefit and accommodation of His Majesty's Governors." Since then it has accommodated a sheep farm, a quarantine station, a racetrack, and a game preserve. Until 1966 it was a military fortification, and it is now under the Coast Guard's jurisdiction. From the ferryboat, it's possible to see two forts—Fort Jay, built in 1798, and Castle Williams, built in 1811—and the Governor's House, dating back to 1708, altered a couple of times since then and the oldest building on the island.

The "Y" also sponsors a tour of the Brooklyn and Staten Island ferry districts, commemorating the anniversary of the first sailing of the Fulton Steam ferry. The tour includes a lecture on the role of ferries in the city's development and a ride on the Staten Island ferry. The tour ends in the Staten Island terminal, with a wine and cheese party.

The **Park Rangers** have a variety of tours and hikes in Staten Island's parks. Call to find out about the variety and the schedule.

The Staten Island Historical Society schedules a three-mile walking tour in Richmondtown, once the center of Staten Island's farmland community. There were mills, dams, a British fort, and a railway here, all of which can still be seen at the Richmondtown Restoration. (The railway is abandoned, of course.) Of twenty-six historic Staten Island buildings, nine have been restored and opened to the public, with exhibits or antique furnishings and textiles. You'll see an old county courthouse, a seventeenth-century school, an antique doll and toy exhibit, a carriage shed filled with old artifacts and fire engines, and a restored museum. For more information about the Richmondtown tour schedules, call 718–351–1617. The restoration project is operated by the Staten Island Historical Society.

Chapter Ten

Novelty Tours

The major institutions and guides with their own firms sometimes undertake tours so original in concept that they cut across neighborhood boundaries to tour artistic and sociological realms or explore facets of New York City's life-styles.

Cy Adler's Shore Walkers has been written about several times in the newspapers, because of a particularly fascinating tour: the pièce de résistance of his firm, in effect. Once a year, on the Saturday during Memorial Day weekend, Mr. Adler leads a walk around Manhattan—approximately thirty-two miles, he estimates. The trek lasts twelve to fourteen hours. He has the group meet at the South Street Seaport at 7 A.M., leads people around the tip of Manhattan, then up the West Side, through pretty parkland along the river, including Riverside Park, to 125th Street. There the group pauses at the Hudson View Diner, a little-known eatery to the general public but a regular stop for truck drivers.

From there, the group heads to Inwood, the northern tip of Manhattan, then turns around and heads back toward the Brooklyn Bridge. Along the way, the group goes through Inwood Park and Highbridge Park. From 155th to 125th streets, coming down the East Side, the hikers encounter no parkland and have no way to get close to the water. They occasionally make their way over difficult terrain, until they end up at the Brooklyn Bridge, "usually as the moon is rising over Brooklyn," says Adler.

Adler is familiar with oceanography (he was hired in 1988 to teach a course in oceanography at the American Museum of Natural History), and so he can talk about the landscape as people hike. They find out that the Hudson River is salt water up to Poughkeepsie, New York, and the East River is a salty tidal estuary, running in two directions twice a day.

Throughout the year, on weekends, Adler leads shorter walks; one of the routes is similar to the 92nd Street "Y"'s route across the Queensboro Bridge to Queens, down to Brooklyn, and back to Manhattan across the Williamsburg Bridge. That walk lasts only six hours.

The **American Institute of Architects** provided a treat for New Yorkers in 1988. Architects gathered in town for a convention, and the architects from the New York chapter of the A.I.A., playing host, led tours to various parts of town. Such rare events are written about in the newspapers in advance, so you can choose your tours before they're sold out. The A.I.A. members also called upon some of the city's leading guides to help with the walks. Versatile Val Ginter worked on the Fifth Avenue "Gold Coast."

Among the 1988 tours were "Queens for Half a Day," "The South Bronx Is Up," "New York City's Subways: Caverns of Culture," "London in New York—a Tour of Manhattan's Public Squares," and "Breakfast at Bloomingdale's." Tours also explored some of the prime examples of twentieth-century architecture in town.

Marvin Gelfand's Walk of the Town takes chartered groups on walks to see the sites of famous crimes; on a "Cops and Robbers" tour; on tours of famous rendezvous of well-known lovers; or on literary tours of the city's neighborhoods to see the places where A. J. Liebling and Damon Runyon, among others, lived, socialized, and worked. Gelfand also conducts a tour of the theater district.

The **Municipal Art Society** also sponsors unusual tours of such places as the Washington Street or Gansevoort meat-market district in the Far

Novelty Tours

West Village, on and near W. 14th Street, and also takes people on the historic sailing ship, *Pioneer,* from the South Street Seaport for a view of the harbor, with a discussion of plans for its future. Similar to the "Y" tour of the Battery Park City area, an M.A.S. walk, led by an architect and preservationist, has taken a group on the piers, discussing the history and possible future uses of the area. (These are just a sampling of the M.A.S.'s "conceptual" tours.

New York University's School of Continuing Education has a program called "The Wonderful World of Food," with tours of stores and restaurants involved in preparing and presenting the city's multi-ethnic cuisines. Tour guides are experts in the various cuisines, ranging from Southern soul food, Cajun, and Tex-Mex, to holiday specialties of the Chinese, Jews, and American Indians, to traditional Eastertime meals. Each section of the course includes a banquet. Some walks go to shops and markets in Greenwich Village; another tour visits Japanese markets and restaurants; another goes to Chinatown during the Chinese New Year celebrations. Another takes you to herbal shops and instructs you in starting your own herb garden.

On one tour, you go to "Little India," usually on Lexington Avenue in the East 20s (though the destination could as easily be E. 6th Street between Second and First avenues) to find out about the culture and cuisine of India. There are also visits to Korean, French, and kosher-style food outlets and restaurants, as well as a wine-buyer's walk for advice about what to buy and how to serve it.

Write to New York University, School of Continuing Education, 331–332 Shimkim Hall, Washington Square, N.Y., N.Y. 10003, for more information about signing up for these tours.

The **92nd Street "Y"** has several creative concepts as the bases for tours that give people the flavor of town. The "Y" has sponsored tours of designers', caterers', and photographers' lofts in the area between Chelsea and Gramercy Park. New York City has inherited from Paris the mantle of the visual-arts capital of the world these days, and the tour introduces people to some of the pace-setters for the city's visual decoration. Arthur Marks has led this tour.

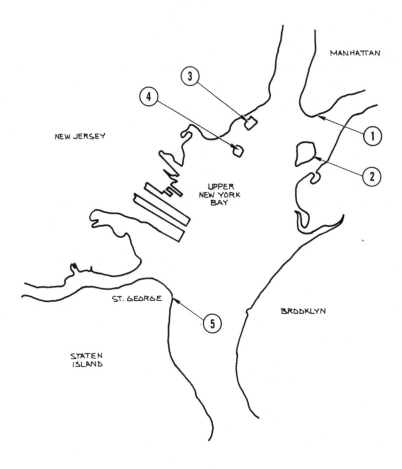

Points of Interest in New York Harbor

1. Ferry terminal in Manhattan
2. Governor's Island
3. Ellis Island
4. Statue of Liberty
5. St. George ferry landing

Novelty Tours

The "Y" also organizes tours of parts of the waterfront. One walk takes people from Bloomingdale's at Lexington Avenue and 60th Street across the Queensboro Bridge, through Long Island City in Queens, and across Newtown Creek and the Pulaski Bridge into Brooklyn. The only similar walk is led by Cy Adler. The group sees Greenpoint and Williamsburg in Brooklyn, two fascinating ethnic neighborhoods, and crosses back to Manhattan over the Williamsburg Bridge. After viewing Manhattan's skyline and the East River, the group stops at Ratner's on the Lower East Side for refreshments.

Another "Y" tour takes people beneath the Whitestone and Throgs Neck bridges on a hike from Flushing Bay to Little Neck Bay at the entrance to Long Island Sound. The walk passes through neighborhoods along the East River. A third waterfront tour goes to the burgeoning southern tip of Manhattan, beginning at the World Trade Center for a stroll along the waterfront esplanade of Battery Park City and the new World Financial Center. The group then takes a ferry to Staten Island for a walk through several Victorian communities—Stapleton, Clifton, and Tompkinsville. Each of these tours lasts about six hours.

The "Y"'s "Behind the Scenes" series can involve a rehearsal with a famous musician at Lincoln Center; a trip to a flower show; a tour of elegant restaurants with their staffs as the lecturers; the Brooklyn Academy of Music; the Park Avenue headquarters of the National Football League; or the studios of Channel 13, the educational television channel, to see how the "MacNeil Lehrer" show, for example, is produced. The "Y" has also sponsored visits to specific people engaged in unusual occupations—for example, a Jewish matchmaker. Another tour seeks out little-known refuges, oases, pocket parks, and atriums, which afford people mini-vacations from the stresses of city living. The "Y," with the biggest walking-tour program in town, comes up with new ideas every season, presented to the "Y" quite often by free-lance guides and then offered to the public.

INDEX

Index

Index

Index

I

Inside New York, 23
Insurance Center Building, 78
Inwood Park, 14, 31–32
"Irish New York," 5, 35, 94, 97, 100, 102
Irving, Washington, 53, 78
Irving Place, 121
Irving Trust Building, 78
Isaac-Hendricks house, 46

J

Jackson Heights, 25, 207
James, Henry, 50
Jazz tours, 142–43, 169–70
Jefferson, Thomas, 84
Jefferson Market Courthouse, 47, 49, 50
Jewish Harlem, 19, 174
"Jewish Life on the Lower East Side" tour, 105
Jewish Urban Study Tours. *See* Schiff, Joseph L.
Jews Alley, 79
Johnson, Philip, 66, 151
John's Pizzeria, 44
Jones, E. Powis, 3, 16

K

Kaplan, James, 23, 74, 80–82
Kebe, Larcelia, 22
Klein's on the Square, 124
Kriskiewicz, John, 15, 184, 194
Kroessler, Jeffrey, 23–24, 32, 82, 96–97, 189, 204–6, 208
Kwong, Peter, Dr., 106

L

Ladies' Mile, 21, 39, 114, 115, 120–34
Lafayette Street, 49, 51, 100
LaGuardia, Fiorello, Mayor, 50

Index

Roosevelt, Theodore, 75, 82, 116, 128, 129, 163
Roosevelt Island, 26, 148
Ross, Rosa, 30, 33, 102–4
Ruggles, Samuel, 114
Runyon, Damon, 7

S

Sal Anthony's restaurant, 115
Salwen, Pete, 33–34, 52–53, 131, 175–77
Sandler, Betty, 98
Schapiro's Winery, 34, 96, 107
Schiff, Joseph L., 5, 34–35, 85–86, 104–5, 177–78, 196
Seagram Building, 26, 138, 151–52
Serbian Orthodox Cathedral of St. Sava, 117, 120, 122, 129
Sheepshead Bay, 15, 18, 186, 189
Shenton, James, Dr., 5, 16, 35, 51, 53, 102, 105–6, 164–65, 196–97,
    203, 208
Sholeen, Joe, 35, 106, 197–99
Shore Walkers of New York, 36, 216–17
Singer, Isaac Bashevis, 95, 99
Singer, Lou, 5, 35–36, 106–7, 199–200
Sniffen Court, 124, 131
Soho, 5–6, 24, 26, 38, 57, 58–63
South Street Seaport, 27, 72, 85
Spanish-Portuguese cemetery, 86
Spence, Ron, 37, 178
St. George's Church, 117
St. Luke's in the Fields, 51
St. Malachy's, 8
St. Mark's-in-the-Bowery, 100, 101–2, 106
St. Mark's Place, 89, 100, 107
St. Patrick's Cathedral, 67
St. Paul's Chapel, 73, 85, 100
St. Peter's Episcopal Church, 118, 121
St. Peter's Lutheran Church, 143, 144
St. Vincent's Hospital, 48

Index

Acknowledgements

I would like to thank all the tour leaders who have shared their expertise to make this book possible. Special thanks go to Libby Corydon, who introduced me to the world of walking tours in New York City. I'd also like to say a special "thank-you" to tour leader Val Ginter, for his painstaking fact-checking of the text and maps.

A special thanks to my typist, Carolyn Sliva, for her painstaking, detailed work and advice.